RESEARCH IN
RACE AND
ETHNIC RELATIONS

Volume 2 • 1980

RESEARCH IN RACE AND ETHNIC RELATIONS

A Research Annual

Editors: CORA BAGLEY MARRETT
Department of Sociology
University of Wisconsin, Madison

CHERYL LEGGON
Department of Sociology
University of Chicago

VOLUME 2 • 1980

A̲i JAI PRESS INC.
Greenwich, Connecticut

CONTENTS

LIST OF CONTRIBUTORS

Michael Banton
Department of Sociology
University of Bristol

Robert Davis
Institute for Research on Poverty
University of Wisconsin, Madison

Jacques Dofny
Department of Sociology
University of Montreal

Darnell F. Hawkins
Department of Sociology
University of North Carolina, Chapel Hill

Charles Hirchman
Department of Sociology
Duke University

Hans-Joachim Hoffman-Nowotny
Department of Sociology
University of Zurich

Vijai P. Singh
Urban Research Center
University of Pittsburgh

INTRODUCTION TO THE VOLUME

CORA BAGLEY MARRETT and CHERYL B. LEGGON

In a pioneering work on intergroup relations, Park (1926: 196) wrote:

> The race relations cycle which takes the form, to state it abstractly, of contact, competition, accommodation, and eventual assimilation, is apparently progressive and irreversible. Customs regulations, immigration restrictions, and racial barriers may slacken the tempo of the movement; may perhaps halt it altogether for a time; but cannot change its direction; cannot, at any rate, reverse it. . . .

Several later analyses highlighted barriers to the rapid absorption of particular groups (Williams, 1947) or proposed cycles that differed from the one which Park developed (see especially Bogardus, 1930, and Brown, 1934). Yet, most of the work undertaken in the next few decades after the Park formulation stressed the inevitably of assimilation. Students of race relations assumed that ascriptive criteria such as race or ethnicity were incompatible with modernization and thus would disappear as industrialization advanced.

One finds a marked change of direction in the current literature. Now emphasized is the persistence of racial and ethnic differences, not only in

Research in Race and Ethnic Relations, Volume 2, pages ix–xii
Copyright © 1980 by JAI Press Inc.
All rights of reproduction in any form reserved.
ISBN: 0-89232-141-5

pre-industrial societies, but in advanced ones as well. Two of the papers in this volume are illustrative. Dofny details the nature of sources of tensions between French Canadians and non-French Canadians in modern Quebec. Hoffman-Nowotny describes the problems surrounding the large community of foreign nationals in Switzerland. These discussions, and an extensive body of materials in other sources, challenge the assumption that conflict over culture or race invariably subsides in complex societies.

The Hoffman-Nowotny analysis illustrates, too, an interest in what might be termed the "public management of intergroup relations." When early writers such as Park, Burgess (Park and Burgess, 1921), or Bogardus (1930) discussed change, they minimized the role of public officials. But in modern societies, relationships among the various ethnic groups might be molded quite significantly by legal actions. In Switzerland, governmental policies on migration affect in important ways the course of relations between the Swiss and the foreign nationals. In India and in the United States, notes Singh, formal policies have been established to redress ethnic group imbalances. But Singh cautions us that official pronouncements against inequality are unlikely to bring about immediate and widespread modifications in long-standing patterns.

An emphasis on the endurance of ethnic and racial divisiveness is evident in some of the concepts now gaining currency among researchers. As Hirschman points out, ethnic stratification models have been popular among those who study ethnic groups. This suggests that analysts are focusing increasingly on the rigidity of ethnic relationships. The concern with *ethnic stratification* rather than with *ethnic differentiation* represents more than a shift in semantics. To understand the significance of the change, let us review the distinction Heller (1969: 3, 4) makes between the terms:

> Social stratification is too often treated as if it were synonymous with social differentiation, which it is not.... [S]tratification [is] a system of structured inequality in the things that count in a given society, that is, both tangible and symbolic goods of that society. The term *structured* indicates an arrangement of elements: the inequality is not random but follows a pattern, displays relative constancy and stability, and is backed by ideas that legitimize and justify it.

As Heller uses the term, stratification is characterized by permanence, by constancy (also see Buckley, 1958). Thus, to speak of ethnic stratification is to raise the possibility that inequalities between groups, and not mere differences, will persist.

But does the existence of racial and ethnic groups in contempoary society demonstrate the tenacity of given social arrangements? The Banton analysis might not so indicate. Banton draws attention to variations in the meanings concepts might have, and argues that the presence of a "racial" group at two contrasting periods need not prove the intractability of racial prejudice. The group designated a race during the first period might in no way resemble the aggregate so designated later.

Banton directs attention to a theme others have pursued: the fluidity of ethnic and racial categories. Studies of ethnic conflict point to the political nature of ethnic identity, noting that not only can it be intensified or weakened, but that it can in fact be created. Bonacich (1979) has made this point with reference to ethnicity in general, and Adekson (1979) and Otite (1979) have documented the phenomenon with reference to Nigerian politics. Such presentations should make students of race and ethnic relations careful in transferring terminology from one time or one setting to another.

Several of the papers in this volume call for greater development of theory in the area of race and ethnic relations; this is true especially of the Hirschman chapter. Hawkins endorses the idea but warns that we must examine the assumptions undergirding the broad frameworks which we adopt. He contends that the study of minority communities has been hampered by the prominence of social structural approaches which regard social elements as highly interrelated. Based on these approaches, he asserts, analysts have thought that the presence of economic insecurity among minority groups necessarily means the existence as well of social and cultural deficiencies.

The Davis analysis has implications for theory development in two ways. First, it shows how theories about minority communities, and especially minority families, can be brought to bear on the study of pathological behavior. Davis asked in his research: Do suicide rates among black Americans vary according to the strength of family ties? Second, the Davis chapter implies that no matter how interested we are in theories about intergroup relations, we should not lose sight of the effects which prejudice and discrimination can have on their victims. The literature within the field falls within two broad traditions: one concerned with racial and ethnic *relations,* the other with *minority* communities. Davis, Hoffman-Nowotny, Hawkins and others summon researchers to link the two traditions in ways which have both theoretical and policy outcomes.

REFERENCES

Adekson, J. Bayo
  1979   "Military organizations in multi-ethnically segmented societies." PP. 109–125

in Research in Race and Ethnic Relations, Volume I, Cora Bagley Marrett and Cheryl Leggon (eds.), Greenwich, Conn. JAI Press.

Bogardus, Emory S.
  1930 "A race-relations cycle," American Journal of Sociology 35:612–617.
Bonacich, Edna
  1979 "The past, present, and future of split labor market theory." Pp. 17–64 in Research in Race and Ethnic Relations, Volume 1, Cora Bagley Marrett and Cheryl Leggon (eds.), Greenwich, Conn. JAI Press.
Brown, W. O.
  1934 "Culture, Contact and race conflict." Pp. 34–37 in Race and Cultural Contacts, E. B. Reuter (ed.), New York: McGraw-Hill.
Buckley, Walter
  1958 "Social stratification and social differentiation." American Sociological Review 23:369–375.
Heller, Celia S.
  1969 Structured Social Inequality. New York: MacMillian.
Otite, Onigu
  1979 "Ethnicity and class in a plural society." Pp: 87–107 in Research and Race and Ethnic Relations, Volume 1, Cora Bagley Marrett and Cheryl Leggon (eds.), Greenwich, Conn. JAI Press.
Park, Robert E.
  1926 "Our racial frontier on the Pacific." Survey Graphic 9.
Park, Robert E. and Ernest W. Burgess
  1921 Introduction to the Science of Sociology. Chicago: University Press of Chicago Press.
Williams, Robin, Jr.
  1947 The Reduction of Intergroup Tensions. Washington, D.C.: Social Science Research Council.

THEORIES AND MODELS OF ETHNIC INEQUALITY

CHARLES HIRSCHMAN

INTRODUCTION

Beginning with the seminal work of Robert Park (1950), there have been numerous efforts to develop sociological theories to classify and explain the variations in ethnic (and racial[1]) inequality over time and space. Yet it is apparent even to the novice that there is no single paradigm that dominates the field. Research findings accumulate, but rarely lead to systematic and cumulative empirical generalizations about the nature and evolution of interethnic relations. There is a wide range of theoretical propositions in the field of race and ethnic relations (Blalock, 1967). Yet few are integrated with larger theory or uniform methods of empirical research. To the extent that schools of research exist, they tend to focus upon common sources of data and analytical methods (historical, attitude surveys, etc.). In this paper, I review the development of a school of

Research in Race and Ethnic Relations, Volume 2, pages 1–20
Copyright © 1980 by JAI Press Inc.
All rights of reproduction in any form reserved.
ISBN: 0-89232-141-5

research that may be emerging as a paradigm for studies of ethnic inequality. I suggest that extensions of what might be called the "models of
ethnic stratification" school can provide a broad analytic framework that
allows for testing some of the classical theoretical questions of changes
and variations in systems of ethnic inequality. Before reviewing the development and directions of this emerging school, I will briefly note some
of the critical limitations of earlier perspectives.

The well-known race relations cycle of Robert Park (later developed
and elaborated by Frazier, 1957) was based on a universal sequence of
stages of interethnic relations, beginning with contact, leading to competition, followed by a period of stable accommodation, and eventuating in
a process of assimilation. Park's bold formulation of a natural history
of ethnic relations was probably the closest approximation to a paradigm of
sociological research on race and ethnic relations. It spawned a series
of studies by Park's students and others to fit the theory to the empirical
world. But the fit was poor in most cases, and a number of conceptual
problems regarding the identification of stages and the transitions between stages led to impasse in further research (Lyman, 1968; for an
alternative assessment, see Geschwender, 1978: Chapter 2).

Other sociologists, most notably Barth and Noel (1972), Lieberson
(1961), Noel (1968), Schermerhorn (1970), Shibutani and Kwan (1965),
and van den Berghe (1967) have put forth theories, most generally in the
form of typologies, to order the field of race and ethnic relations. But it
seems fairly clear that none of these theoretical perspectives have become
paradigms in the sense of leading a dominant research tradition. The
obstacles to cumulative research based on these alternative perspectives
have been the difficulties of operationalizing basic concepts and of finding appropriate data to test emergent hypotheses. In general, the basic
relationships in these different theories are expressed in fairly abstract
terms and are then illustrated with examples from a few societies. What is
to be explained—interethnic stratification, political or economic dominance, assimilation or lack of it—varies considerably between and within
theoretical perspectives, and it is often assumed that these quite different
dimensions all co-vary together.

The basic kernel of most macro-sociological theories of ethnic inequality is that the type and organization of society shape the structure of
ethnic relations. And as societies are transformed in various ways, ethnic
relations are posited to change or evolve in certain directions. Other
factors such as the relative size of majority and minority groups, the
nature of the encounter (migration, conquest), and initial distribution of

power (military, economic) are additional contingencies that affect the outcome. How to put all these ideas into a systematic framework to guide research is the awesome task. First of all, the lack of comparable data for historical-comparative research is enough to deter all but the most gifted or foolhardy investigators. Moreover, what are the dimensions or characteristics of societies that might shape ethnic structures? Is it industrialization, the type of polity, who owns the means of production, Western tradition or racism that is the key to the puzzle? These are some of the central variables in the varied theories of race and ethnic relations. At the present time it seems that no consensus has emerged and the field remains eclectic in its orientation.

Premature closure of the widely varied research on race and ethnic relations into a common framework may not be universally regarded as a positive achievement. Diversity has its uses, especially in the search for an understanding of the nature and causes of social phenomena. But there are real gains to be had from cumulative science as well. Within a broad paradigm of research that encompasses elements of theory and a framework for empirical inquiry, it is possible to take many aspects of the research endeavor for granted and to concentrate on replications and extensions of empirical investigation. It is not necessary for each scientist to develop a new theory or strategy for research, but rather there is an emphasis on elaboration of the underlying theory and critical empirical tests of emergent hypotheses. It is the thesis of this paper that research in the field of race and ethnic relations has, over the past decade, begun to gravitate around a perspective, labeled here as ''models of ethnic stratification.'' This ''emergent paradigm'' has yet to become dominant, but the basic perspective has been widely diffused, and it seems appropriate to take stock of its background, emergence, and potential for cumulative research in the field.

''Models of ethnic stratification'' are not really theories in the mold of linking social structure and ethnic relations, as did those cited in the opening paragraphs of this paper. Indeed the framework has been exceedingly narrow, basically measuring and interpreting interethnic socioeconomic inequality, typically in terms of income, occupation, and education. The interpretation is founded on causal models, estimated with multivariate regression techniques, that measure how social background characteristics affect differential socioeconomic achievement. While most of the research to date has not spoken to the broad issues raised by the classical theories, there are clear signs that the widening scope of empirical studies using the basic model of ethnic inequality is leading in

4   CHARLES HIRSCHMAN

directions that address some of the broader questions of the linkages between social change, social organization, and ethnic inequality. These topics will be addressed in the following review of models of ethnic inequality.

PRE-MODEL FORMULATIONS

It has always been tempting to interpret measures of ethnic inequality as indicators of discrimination, the degree to which members of disadvantaged groups are confined to a subordinate position solely on the basis of their ascribed status—race or ethnicity. Yet apologists for the existing social order could simply argue that ethnic disparities were due to differences on other criteria that determined socioeconomic success such as education, mental ability, or minority concentrations in depressed geographic areas. Thus, there was (and remains) a great scientific interest in measuring what fraction of ethnic inequality is due to discrimination. Perhaps the single most influential article along these lines was Siegel's (1965). Using the standard statistical methods of controlling for population composition between two populations (Kitagawa, 1955), Siegel was able to estimate how much of the gross income differences between white and black men in the United States would remain if both races had exactly the same distributions by region of residence, education, and occupation. His results showed that most of black-white income inequality was not due to differences in occupation, education, or region, but something else—most likely discrimination. Siegel noted that differences in education, occupation, and region (the control variables) might also reflect discrimination. As a first step, his study presented a basic, though somewhat cumbersome, analytic framework for the interpretation of ethnic inequality.

Another pioneering study along these lines was Lieberson and Fuguitt's (1966) application of Markov chain techniques to estimate the separate effects of social origins and social mobility on black-white occupational differences. By noting that differences in the distribution of black and white men by occupation can be algebraically separated into vectors of social origins (father's occupation) and matrices of mobility (from father's to son's occupation), it is possible to hold one factor constant and vary the other. Lieberson and Fuguitt discovered that black-white occupational inequality would virtually disappear in a couple of generations if discrimination were to be eliminated (equivalent mobility matrices).[2] Clearly discrimination, indexed by unequal achievement among persons with equivalent backgrounds, has long been the primary cause of racial inequality in American society.

The basic question of the differential effects of social background variables and the residual differences between ethnic groups due to discrimination can be more adequately addressed in a broader multivariate framework that formalizes both the implicit theory and the basic methods of investigation.

BASIC ETHNIC STRATIFICATION MODELS

The recent development of models within the field of social stratification can be dated from 1967 with the publication of Blau and Duncan's *The American Occupational Structure*. By transposing the question of social mobility into a multivariate analysis of the socioeconomic life cycle with the aid of statistical/theoretical technique of path analysis (Duncan, 1966), a new school of social research emerged. This new school could not do everything, and indeed, many of the classic questions of social stratification were beyond its purview. But the study of the impact of parental socioeconomic status upon son's socioeconomic position—the question of social mobility—was broadened and reinvigorated.

Perhaps the major contribution of the new stratification school was the possibility for the accumulation of knowledge via replication and extension of the basic models. The statistics of multiple regression allow for the incorporation of additional independent variables, but the rigor of path models required that the relationship of each new independent variable to all other variables be posited in advance and interpreted in a causal framework. Since the notion of the socioeconomic life cycle provides a temporal ordering of most variables, this was not a major obstacle. Duncan and his students were keenly aware of the possibilities for extension of the basic stratification model to include many other relevant variables (Duncan, Featherman, Duncan, 1972). These early studies included analyses of the factors accounting for inequality between blacks and whites (Blau and Duncan, 1967: Ch. 6; Duncan, 1969) and among other American ethnic groups (Duncan and Duncan, 1968). The application of models of the intergenerational process of stratification to ethnic inequality made for a more thorough investigation of the questions raised in the Siegel and Lieberson-Fuguitt analyses, yet also raised some new issues. This can be most clearly seen in the models and analysis presented in Duncan's (1969) classic article "Inheritance of Poverty or Inheritance of Race?."

The path diagrams in Figure 1 show the basic model of the

Figure 1. Models of Stratification Among Black and White Men, Based upon 1962 Occupational Change in a Generation (OCG) Survey.

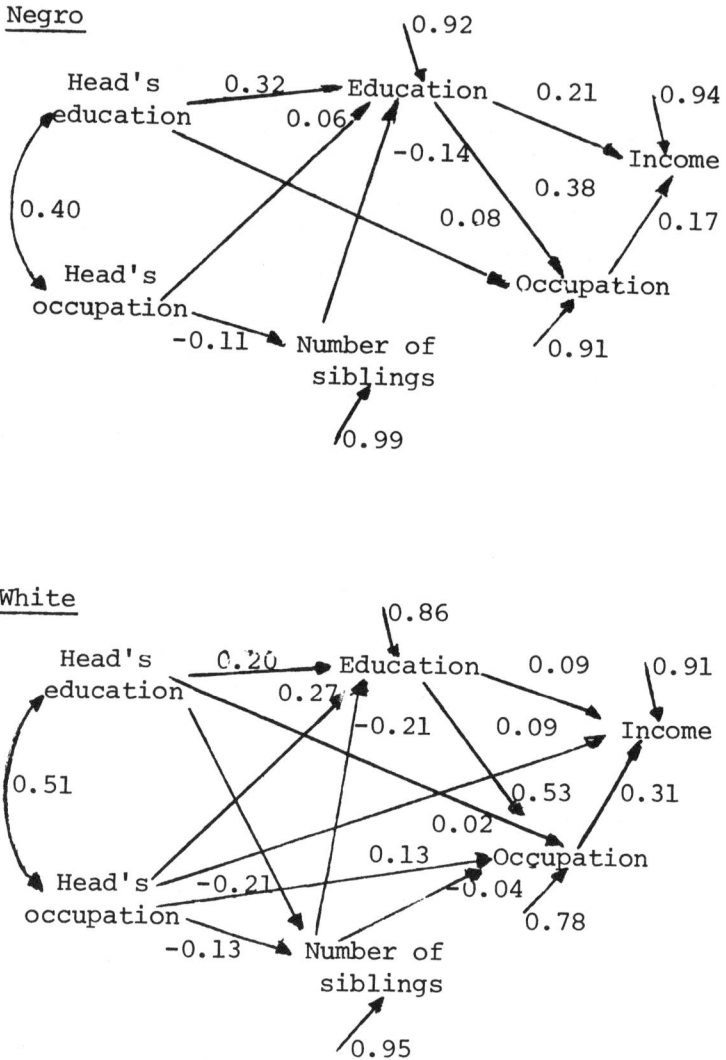

Source: Duncan, 1969, p. 90 (Figure 4-1).

socioeconomic life cycle separately for black and white men based upon the 1962 Occupational Change in a Generation Survey data (see Duncan, 1969, for more detail). This schematic presentation of the results of multiple regression equations with coefficients in standardized form is designed to facilitate causal interpretation. Straight lines indicate unidirectional causal lines, while curved lines represent unanalyzed joint associations between exogenous variables. What is immediately obvious from this form of presentation (that is not in the usual multiple regression analysis) is that outcome variables are dependent not only on direct (or net) effects from prior variables but also upon indirect effects that are mediated by intervening variables. Thus the "model" (it need not be of a path analysis type) uses the statistical techniques to test the causal/ theoretical framework, not vice versa.

Since the intention here is exposition of an approach, not interpretation of substance, I will not elaborate extensively upon the content of Figure 1. Basically, it shows the relationships between socioeconomic background and socioeconomic attainment among black and white men. But it does not directly address the handicap of black men in the American stratification system. This requires combining the information on differential racial translation of background into attainment (standardized regression coefficients in Figure 1) with the racial differentials in socioeconomic background resources. Duncan ties these together in statistical "experiments" by controlling the racial inequality in various social background variables, such as father's occupation, etc., and observing the effects upon racial inequality in attainment (black means on background variables are entered into the regression equations for whites). He concludes that the major source of racial inequality is not the poorer social background or education of blacks, but the poorer rewards that society provides blacks with equivalent backgrounds and qualifications as whites. Thus it is not the "inheritance of poverty" that most limits the socioeconomic success of blacks, but the recurrent discrimination that each successive generation encounters (inheritance of race).

Duncan's clear exposition of how to "model" and interpret racial/ ethnic differences in stratification has greatly influenced contemporary studies of this topic. But some observers have pointed out that the statistical decomposition of racial/ethnic inequality using regression techniques actually leads to more complexity than Duncan's neat interpretation suggests (Winsborough and Dickinson, 1971; Althauser and Wigler, 1972). Specifically, decomposition procedures can reveal at least four empirical factors: (1) inequality due to differences in social background, e.g., means on independent variables, (2) differences in slopes, the regressions of the dependent variables on the independent variables, (3) differences in the intercept values, whose value is constant over all categories of the independent variables (basically the residual term), and (4) statistical interactions between race and other relationships in the model. The problem is that these factors are not necessarily conceptually or empirically distinct. Recall that the original objective underlying these basic investigations was to separate inequality into two interpretable factors: those due to discrimination, and those due to other factors. As noted earlier, differences in social background (composition in Siegel's work or means on independent variables in the regression models) may actually be due to the legacy of discrimination from earlier generations. But the other components are problematic in their interpretation as well.

While it might be useful to label intercept differences as discrimination that affects all members of the disadvantaged groups and differences in slopes as discrimination that varies in degree depending on the values on an independent variable, the empirical distinction between these terms in any equation is partially a function of the assignment of a zero value on the independent variable. The statistical "interaction" appears in the different component solutions, depending on which standard population is used in equations in the statistical experiments (Althauser and Wigler, 1972). In Duncan's analysis the interaction component is averaged into one or more of the other components. Winsborough and Dickinson (1971) show how to estimate it separately, but its interpretation remains opaque.

A statistically equivalent method of the basic model of ethnic inequality is to run ethnic/race categories as separate variables (as dummy variables in binary coding) in a single equation (Duncan and Duncan, 1968; Duncan and Featherman, 1972; Hirschman, 1975). The typical sequence of analytical steps in this procedure is somewhat different than in Duncan's example. A brief illustration of the series of basic equations in such an analysis might best convey the ideas and techniques that are part of the process of model building.

First, a basic equation with only the dependent variable regressed upon the categories of the ethnic variable is estimated:

$$Y = a + b_1E \tag{1}$$

where Y is an occupational attainment variable, measured in an interval scale and E represents a series of dummy variables, one for each category of the ethnic/race classification. The associated regression coefficients, represented by b_1, would be the gross effects of ethnicity on occupational attainment. These coefficients can be adjusted to deviations from the grand mean of the dependent variable, and thus would be exactly the same as differences between the average occupational attainment of each ethnic group.[3] This simple model is then expanded to include other background variables such as Father's Occupation, Father's Education, Number of Siblings, etc. For instance, consider the equation:

$$Y = a + b_1E + b_2F + b_3A \tag{2}$$

where Y and E are the same as before, F is Father's Occupation, and A is the educational attainment of the respondent. The change in the ethnic effects (b_1) from Model 1 to Model 2 is due to the differential distribution of the ethnic groups by Father's Occupation and Education. The resulting net ethnic coefficients in Model 2 are the effects not mediated by or associated with the two other variables. The form of the equation in Model 2 assumes additive relationships between Education and Father's Occupation and Occupational Attainment across ethnic groups.

To test the hypothesis of different slopes of occupation on education among the different ethnic communities, it is necessary to expand the basic model with additional interaction terms. This is shown in Model 3:

$$Y = a + b_1E + b_2F + b_3A = b_4EA \tag{3}$$

where all variables are as before and EA represents a series of dummy variables of each ethnic category times the education variable. If the variance explained by Model 3 is significantly greater than that of Model 2, one can interpret the b_4 coefficients as the impact of differential educational slopes on occupation, net of the additive educational variable.

Even with only a few independent variables, this sort of model building can quickly become very complicated in both the statistical models and in the interpretation of results. Yet the basic ideas that underlie such an approach remain rather straightforward. The underlying question is always the same: What social background characteristics explain the differential socioeconomic attainment of ethnic groups? Part of the effects of differential social background may represent the legacy of past discrimination while the unexplained residual differences are due to other factors—most likely discrimination in the socioeconomic achievement process. This approach can also be used to address whether differential socioeconomic attainments by ethnic communities are mediated by or uniquely due to social psychological variables such as ambition. The empirical assessments of this hypothesis in American society have not supported the widespread belief that differential cultural orientations across ethnic communities account for their varying degrees of socioeconomic success (Featherman, 1971; Duncan and Featherman, 1972).

EXTENSIONS OF MODELS OF ETHNIC STRATIFICATION

The models of ethnic stratification described above, however elaborate, do not address the core issues raised by some of grander theories of race and ethnic relations. First, these models only address one aspect of ethnic relations—socioeconomic inequality.[4] Moreover, these models only specify the relative impact of social background variables on inequality and provide indirect measures of specific forms of discrimination. The content of the grander theories specified (or attempted to specify) the societal conditions or social structure that gave rise to relationships between ethnicity and other variables and changes in these relationships. Of course, the lack of standardized methodology to accompany these theories has greatly inhibited their potential impact on cumulative empirical research. However, it is possible to extend the basic models with longitudinal and comparative data to address some aspects of the broader theoretical issues. I will outline the direction of these extensions, first considering models of changes in ethnic inequality over time, and second, the comparative analysis of social structure upon ethnic inequality.

Changes in Ethnic Stratification

In spite of the diminished position of Park's original race relations cycle hypothesis, the eventual end-state of assimilation has remained a useful empirical expectation for trends of ethnic inequality. The hypothesis is that modernization and industrialization will gradually weaken the importance of ethnic, racial, and other ascriptive criteria, and lead to a stratification system with an emphasis on achieved characteristics. The logic of this hypothesis clearly rests on the assumption that industrial society has certain functional needs that can only be satisfied by rational decision making (for the classic exposition, see Kerr, Dunlop, Harbison, and Myers, 1964), and that discrimination on the basis of religion, language, and ethnicity are primordial sentiments which are counterproductive and will diminish over time. This hypothesis is implicit in the considerable literature on "structural assimilation" and "institutional disparation" (Taeuber and Taeuber, 1965; Eisenstadt, 1953; Lieberson, 1963). Although not directly focused upon ethnic stratification, Treiman's (1970) arguments in his summary of propositions dealing with the process of stratification during the course of industrialization clearly support the thesis that ethnicity and race, like all other ascriptive criteria, will become less important as determinants of socioeconomic achievement as economic development proceeds.

The "rise of ethnicity" including persistent racial and ethnic divisions in post-industrial societies has given pause to some of the more general assumptions of this school of thought—that industrialization will weaken the structure of ethnic inequality (see Glazer and Moynihan, 1970;

Greeley, 1974). There is also a counter-literature that questions the general thesis on both theoretical and empirical grounds. Blumer (1965) strongly challenged the hypothesis that industrialization will necessarily lead to a reduction of racial/ethnic inequality or conflict. He contended it would be more likely that the structure of industrialization will adapt to the existing racial institutions and mores rather than the other way around. Other theoretical perspectives posit that social change leads to growing interethnic conflict and competition as traditional arrangements break down (van den Berghe, 1967). It is possible to argue that social change will bring both greater interethnic conflict and a weakening of the structures of ethnic inequality.

Another important challenge comes from Marxist critics who have formulated alternative theoretical perspectives that specify how ethnic divisions can be maintained and strengthened through the normal processes of uneven capitalist development. These critics have argued theoretically and demonstrated empirically that ethnic and racial inequality can be long maintained and even institutionalized in industrial-capitalist societies via structures of regional inequality and segmented labor markets (Bonacich, 1972, 1976; Hechter, 1971, 1974). These ideas seem sure to inspire considerable empirical research in the coming years.

At present the debate over the consequences of industrialization on ethnic inequality is pretty much of a standoff. A plausible theoretical case can be made for either interpretation, and selective evidence can be brought to bear in support of both sides. While it would be premature to suggest that this debate over the effects of social change on ethnic stratification can be resolved with the models described in the previous section, it is clearly possible to measure trends in ethnic stratification systems. For instance, to the extent that the net effects of ethnicity (an indicator of discrimination) on socioeconomic status decrease over time, one might argue that the system is becoming "blind" with respect to ethnic status—thus supporting the industrialization thesis. Or if the differential slopes of occupation on education across ethnic communities persist undiminished, then one might question the convergence or assimilation hypothesis.

The fundamental prerequisite for such assessments of changes in ethnic stratification (or any study of social change) is comparable data for two or more time points. A significant study in this regard has been Featherman and Hauser's (1976) analysis of changes in racial stratification in the United States from 1962 to 1973. With the aid of replicated survey data, they examined the socioeconomic origins and attainments of blacks and whites of successive cohorts, holding age constant. They found modest evidence in support of the industrialization thesis, with the process of stratification among young black men becoming quite similar to that of young white men in recent years. Convergence was still far from being realized and changes were minimal among older age groups, but movement in the hypothesized direction had clearly occurred. It can be anticipated that work along these lines will expand and models will be refined in the coming years. There is already a tremendous scientific and policy interest in the trend in black-white inequality in the United States (Farley and Hermalin, 1972; Farley, 1977), and the growing availability of comparable time-series data will certainly spark creative attempts to formally "model" the dynamics of ethnic change (Winsborough, 1975; Mason, Taeuber, and Winsborough, 1977).

Even if these longitudinal models succeed in documenting changes (or nonchange) in ethnic stratification systems over time in the United States or other societies, we will still be left with uncertainty over the reasons for the change. It may be possible to rule out some explanations, by noting the relative impact of various variables in the models. For instance, changes in the composition of social origins of ethnic/racial groups does not require any reference to societal changes that affected the education-occupation-income relationships of adults in the population. But if discrimination (intercepts and slopes) seems to have lessened its impact, there are a wide variety of competing explanations—a tightening labor market, government policies to restrict discrimination, or the growth of jobs in new sectors. Clearly, the links between social structure and ethnic stratification can only be indirectly examined through trend analysis. But there are ways to build models with explicit links between social structure and ethnic inequality.

Comparative Models of Ethnic Stratification

The plea for comparative research is one of the frequent, but neglected tasks within sociology, and in the social sciences generally. The basic requirement for comparative research is comparable data from different societies or communities. For researchers who work within a quantitative research orientation, as exemplified in the model construction strategy, this requirement is almost never satisfied. Even in rare cases, when comparative quantitative analysis is attempted, the comparisons are limited to a small number of cases, two, three, or four societies. Since different patterns in two countries may result from an almost infinite variety of other societal differences, explanations are always speculative. The situation is much like that of trend analysis, where differences can be described, some explanations can be ruled out, but conclusive explanations (linkages of social structure to patterns of ethnic stratification) remain rare.

However, a within nation approach to comparative analysis, using models of ethnic stratification, is possible with the dissemination of massive data files, such as large samples from national censuses. Such large data files make it possible to divide the population into a number of meaningful geographical areas that vary along structural characteristics that may affect the process of socioeconomic attainment among ethnic communities.

The rationale for this form of comparative analysis is rooted in the logic of sociological reasoning. While individual outcomes such as socioeconomic achievement are partially the function of individual characteristics, there are likely to be major influences from the institutional framework of the society or community as well. In fact, much of the interpretation of relationships in the basic models are couched in terms of how individual characteristics are evaluated by the social institutions in society. For instance, the differential effect of social background on achievement between ethnic groups is usually interpreted as institutional discrimination (by employers, supervisors, and other gate keepers). If social processes such as discrimination vary among communities, comparative research can specify both the magnitude of variation and the structural characteristics associated with the degree of variation.

The implicit hypothesis in the comparative analysis of ethnic inequality is that some institutional structures foster more egalitarian stratification process, with less emphasis on color and ethnic identity. Patterns of ethnic discrimination are intertwined with processes of mobility into and through schools, employing institutions and other organizations that affect socioeconomic achievement.

In a sense, this type of work is already part of mainstream sociological research with the use of ecological variables. For instance, size of place of residence (or size of birthplace) is a critical variable that is associated with availability of opportunities. Larger towns and cities are thought to provide more opportunities based upon achieved, rather than ascribed characteristics relative to small towns and rural areas (although empirical studies cast doubt on this hypothesis, see Mueller, 1977). The introduction of geographical variables always requires a simultaneous consideration of migration, for the effects of a community may be different for in-migrants and natives. In addition to size of place, the most common

ecological variable is region. Studies of racial inequality in the United
States have shown that patterns varied considerably between the South
and the non-South (Hogan and Featherman, 1977).

But the possibilities for inclusion of the ecological effects of social
structure go far beyond just measures of urbanization and region. With
extremely large data files, it is possible to create contextual variables of
community structure that may influence the patterns of ethnic stratification. The appropriate geographical unit may vary according to the
availability of data and the type of hypothesis, but metropolitan areas
which closely approximate labor markets may be the most appropriate
choice for studies of stratification processes. By constructing contextual
variables of community structure, such as size, growth, or industrial
structure, the investigator can specify and directly measure the impact of
social structural variables upon ethnic stratification systems. The strategy
of model-building for such analyses is akin to the previous efforts of
measuring the effects of neighborhoods and schools upon academic
achievement (Sewell and Armer, 1966; Hauser, 1969, 1971). While the
variables would be quite different, the logic and methods of incorporating
both individual social background variables and ecological variables in
the same models are similar.

The idea of incorporating ecological characteristics into models of
ethnic inequality is not an original one. There is a long tradition of
research that seeks to explain black-white disparities in terms of the
relative size of the minority population in the community (Blalock, 1957;
Brown and Fuguitt, 1972; Frisbie and Neidert, 1977). In their analysis of
development towns in Israel, Spilerman and Habib (1976) point out that
the industry structure of towns shapes the distribution of occupational
opportunities. And if ethnic groups are differentially distributed across
towns, as is the case almost everywhere, ethnic inequality is partially a
function of community characteristics. In a similar vein, Yancey et al.
(1976) offer a revisionist perspective on ethnicity among European immigrants to the United States. They argue that ethnicity is largely a function
of the structural conditions of American cities at the time of their arrival.
Different immigrant-ethnic groups are often tied into a particular
industrial-occupational structure (and associated culture) as a result of the
opportunities that were available in the places and times in which they
settled.

The formalization of a research strategy using community contextual
variables in models of ethnic inequality is still incomplete. While prior
studies point to community size and relative minority size as important
structural factors, the interpretation of these variables and the incorpora-

tion of others is open to debate. Among the possibilities for further research are such structural features as recent migration to the community, percent of employment in manufacturing, and the percent of the adult population with post-secondary education. Migration may indicate that domestic labor was insufficient for employment growth, and it was necessary to attract workers from elsewhere. Such a situation of labor demand may weaken traditional patterns of discrimination against minority workers. Similarly, the growth of manufacturing employment may act as a force to minimize ethnic barriers. It is widely believed that ethnic bars to industrial employment are less than in other sectors of the economy. Communities with a sizable share of the work force in manufacturing activities may be less able to maintain informal criteria based upon status or ethnicity in hiring and promotion than other communities. Another provocative hypothesis is that communities with a higher level of educational attainment will be less likely to institutionalize ethnic discrimination. The reasoning would be based upon the assumption that higher education weakens beliefs that legitimate discriminatory practices. These are only some of the possibilities for hypothesis testing within this framework. With some ingenuity it would be feasible to include contextual variables from a wide variety of other data sources. Some examples might be: the level of government expenditures, the presence and activities of affirmative action programs, variations in minoirty groups political activity, and the strength of labor unions. The great virtue of this framework is its openness to a wide scope of variables that may represent quite different (and opposing) theoretical perspectives.

There is an empirical possibility that most cities in the United States are so similar in terms of labor market diversity that community effects will be insignificant. In fact, one recent study reported there was too little intercity variation in black-white inequality in the United States to merit further inquiry (Stolzenberg and D'Amico, 1977), but both the theoretical and empirical questions remain in dispute (Spilerman and Miller, 1977).

One might argue that the comparative analysis of communities on regions within one country will hold constant many of the critical structural variables that shape stratification systems—namely, political institutions. This limitation is clearly acknowledged, but that should not be an argument against pursuing research on community effects within societies.

CONCLUSIONS

Theories of racial and ethnic relations have been plentiful, but the empirical testing of hypotheses has not led to a cumulative growth of knowledge. Disparate research findings from various studies increase in number, but do not seem to bear much relationship to one another. It is obvious that a strong paradigm of research has not emerged. But the growth of empirical studies of racial/ethnic inequality in the United States over the last decade suggests that formal models of the process of stratification may be a significant turning point in the development of the field.

Not only do such models offer a rigorous statistical method of analysis, but a cumulative research tradition seems to be developing. The more simple models were formulated to measure the relative amount of discrimination in overall measures of inequality. But the expansion of these models to include social origins and a full temporal ordering of the socioeconomic career required a causal specification and interpretation of how ethnic inequality is generated and transmitted across and within generations.

The "openness" of such models to the inclusion of other variables, and the requirement of a theoretical rationale for each relationship between variables in the system, encourages the development of a cumulative research strategy. The two major frontiers of research on ethnic stratification within this emergent paradigm are trend and comparative analysis. Trend analysis will speak to the question of whether there is a growing convergence in ethnic stratification, as suggested by the hypothesis that modernization leads to assimilation. While the extensions of models of inequality to temporal changes will show the mechanisms whereby inequality is maintained or reduced, it may not measure the direct links of social structure upon the stratification process.

But via comparative analysis, one can specify certain attributes of the social structure of geographical areas or cities that may affect the levels and processes of ethnic stratification. Such studies are increasingly possible with the availability of very large data files to measure geographic areas and ecological characteristics. In another decade or so, we may see development of a strong research paradigm for the study of race and ethnic stratification.

ACKNOWLEDGMENT

This is a revised version of a paper presented at the 1978 Annual meetings of the American Sociology Association. I thank Monica Boyd, Richard Campbell, Alan Kerckhoff, Judah Matras, and Ronald Rindfuss for their constructive comments on an earlier draft of this manuscript, and Teresa Dark for typing it. This paper is part of a research project, "Social Change and Ethnic Inequality" (MH 30663) supported by the National Institute of Mental Health.

NOTES

1. Much of the prior literature is phrased in terms of race; I prefer the more general term, ethnicity, which has fewer pejorative interpretations. Depending on prior usage by other authors, I will use the two terms interchangeably.

2. Thus illustrating the principle of weak ergodicity, a familiar idea to statisticians. For an overview of the potential applications of the matrix equation representation of social mobility, see Matras (1967).

3. The statistical technique for doing this is Multiple Classification Analysis, a form of multiple regression that incorporates categorical predicator variables. The method is presented in Melichar (1965). A computer program for this form of statistical analysis is documented in Andrews et al. (1975).

4. While other dimensions of interethnic relations such as conflict and ethnic identity may be closely intertwined with inequality, the analytical restriction to only inequality measures as dependent variables enhances the possibility of a standardized methodology.

REFERENCES

Althauser, Robert P. and Michael Wigler
  1972   "Standardization and component analysis." Sociological Methods and Research 1:97-135.
Andrews, Frank M., James N. Morgan, John A. Sonquist, and Laura Klem
  1975   Multiple Classification Analysis: A Report on a Computer Program for Multiple Regression Using Categorical Predictors. 2nd ed. Ann Arbor, Mich.: Institute for Social Research.
Barth, Ernest and Donald Noel
  1972   "Conceptual frameworks for the analysis of race relations: an evaluation." Social Forces 50 (March):333-348.
Blalock, Hubert M.
  1957   "Percent nonwhite and discrimination in the South." American Sociological Review 22 (December):677-682.
  1967   Toward a Theory of Minority Group Relations. New York: Wiley.
Blau, Peter and Otis Dudley Duncan
  1967   The American Occupational Structure. New York: Wiley.
Blumer, Herbert
  1965   "Industrialization and race relations." Pp. 220-253 in Guy Hunter (ed.), Industrialization and Race Relations. London: Oxford University Press.
Bonacich, Edna
  1972   "A theory of ethnic antagonism: the split labor market." American Sociological Review 37:547-559.
  1976   "Advanced capitalism and black/white relations in the United States." American Sociological Review 41:34-51.
Brown, David L. and Glenn V. Fuguitt
  1972   "Percent nonwhite and racial disparity in nonmetropolitan cities in the South." Social Science Quarterly 53 (December):573-582.
Duncan, Beverly and Otis Dudley Duncan

1968   "Minorities and the process of stratification." American Sociological Review
        20:210-217.
Duncan, Otis Dudley
1966   "Path analysis: sociological examples." American Journal of Sociology 72
        (July):1-16.
1969   "Inheritance of poverty or inheritance of race?" Pp. 85-110 in Daniel P.
        Moynihan (ed.), On Understanding Poverty: Perspectives from the Social Sci-
        ences. New York: Basic Books.
Duncan, Otis Dudley and David Featherman
1972   "Psychological and cultural factors in the process of occupational achieve-
        ment." Social Science Research 1 (June):121-145.
Duncan, Otis Dudley, David Featherman, and Beverly Duncan
1972   Socioeconomic Background and Achievement. New York: Seminar Press.
Eisenstadt, S. N.
1953   "Analysis of patterns of immigration and absorption of immigrants." Popula-
        tion Studies 7 (November):167-180.
Farley, Reynolds
1977   "Trends in racial inequalities: have the gains of the 1900s disappeared in the
        1970s?" American Sociological Review 42:189-207.
Farley, Reynolds and Albert Hermalin
1972   "The 1960s: a decade of progress for blacks." Demography 9:353-370.
Featherman, David
1971   "The socioeconomic achievement of white religio-ethnic subgroups: social and
        psychological explanations." American Sociological Review 36 (April):207-
        222.
Featherman, David and Robert M. Hauser
1976   "Changes in the socioeconomic stratification of the races, 1962-1973." Ameri-
        can Journal of Sociology 82:621-651.
Frazier, E. Franklin
1957   Race and Culture Contacts in the Modern World. Boston: Beacon Press.
Frisbie, W. Parker and Lisa Neidert
1977   "Inequality and the relative size of minority populations: a comparative
        analysis." American Journal of Sociology 82 (March):1007-1030.
Geschwender, James A.
1978   Racial Stratification in America. Dubuque, Iowa: W. C. Brown.
Glazer, Nathan and Daniel P. Moynihan
1970   Beyond the Melting Pot. 2nd ed. Cambridge: MIT Press.
Greeley, Andrew
1974   Ethnicity in the United States: A Preliminary Reconnaissance. New York:
        Wiley.
Hauser, Robert M.
1969   "Schools and the stratification process." American Journal of Sociology 74:
        586-611.
1971   Socioeconomic Background and Educational Performance. Arnold M. and
        Caroline Rose Monograph. Washington, D.C.: American Sociological Associa-
        tion.

Hechter, Michael
1971   "Towards a theory of ethnic change." Politics and Society 5:21-44.
1974   "The political economy of ethnic change." American Journal of Sociology 79:1151-1178.
Hirschman, Charles
1975   Ethnic and Social Stratification in Peninsular Malaysia. Rose Monograph Series. Washington, D.C.: American Sociological Association.
Hogan, Denis P. and David L. Featherman
1977   "Racial stratification and socioeconomic change in the American North and South." American Journal of Sociology 83:100-126.
Kerr, Clark, John T. Dunlop, Frederick Harbison, and Charles A. Myers
1964   Industrialism and Industrial Man. New York: Oxford University Press.
Kitagawa, E. M.
1955   "Components of a difference between two rates." Journal of the American Statistical Association 50:1168-1194.
Lieberson, Stanley
1961   "A societal theory of race and ethnic relations." American Sociological Review 26:902-910.
1963   Ethnic Patterns in American Cities. New York: Free Press.
Lieberson, Stanley and Glenn Fuguitt
1966   "Negro-white occupational differences in the absence of discrimination." American Journal of Sociology 75:188-200.
Lyman, Stanford
1968   "The race relations cycle of Robert Park." Pacific Sociological Review 11:16-22.
Mason, William M., Karl E. Taeuber, and Halliman H. Winsborough (eds).
1977   Old Data for New Research: Report of a Workshop on Research Opportunities and Issues in the Design and Construction of Public Use Samples from the 1940 and 1950 Censuses and from Current Population Surveys from 1960 Foreword, Held in Madison, Wisconsin, June 28-30, 1976. Center for Demography and Ecology, University of Wisconsin, Madison.
Matras, Judah
1967   "Social mobility and social structure: some insights from the linear model." American Sociological Review 32:608-614.
Melichar, Emanuel
1965   "Least squares analysis of economic survey data." American Statistical Association. Proceedings of the Business and Economic Statistics Section:373-385.
Mueller, Charles
1977   "Socioeconomic achievements and city size." Pp. 249-270 in Robert M. Hauser and David L. Featherman, The Process of Stratification: Trends and Analyses. New York: Academic Press.
Noel, Donald
1968   "A theory of the origin of ethnic stratification." Social Problems 16 (Fall):152-172.

Park, Robert
1950   Race and Culture. Glencoe, Ill.: Free Press.
Schermerhorn, Richard A.
1970   Comparative Ethnic Relations. New York: Random House.
Siegel, Paul
1965   "On the cost of being a Negro." Sociological Inquiry 35:41-59.
Sewell, William H. and Michael Armer
1966   "Neighborhood context and college plâns." American Sociological Review 31:159-168.
Shibutani, Tamotsu and Kian M. Kwan
1965   Ethnic Stratification: A Comparative Approach. New York: Macmillan.
Spilerman, Seymour and Jack Habib
1976   "Development towns in Israel: the role of community in creating ethnic disparities in labor force characteristics." American Journal of Sociology 81: 781-812.
Spilerman, Seymour and Richard E. Miller
1977   "City nondifferences revisited." American Sociological Review 42:979-983.
Stolzenberg, Ross M. and Ronald J. D'Amico
1977   "City differences and nondifferences in the effect of race and sex on occupational distribution." American Sociological Review 42:937-950.
Taeuber, Karl E. and Alma F. Taeuber
1965   "The Negro as an immigrant group." American Journal of Sociology 69:374-382.
Treiman, Donald J.
1970   "Industrialization and social stratification." Pp. 207-234 in Edward O. Laumann (ed.), Social Stratification: Research and Theory for the 1970s. Indianapolis: Bobbs-Merrill.
van den Berghe, Pierre
1967   Race and Racism: A Comparative Perspective. New York: Basic Books.
Winsborough, H. H.
1975   "Age, period, cohort and education effects on earnings by race." Pp. 201-217 in Kenneth C. Land and Seymour Spilerman (eds.), Social Indicator Models. New York: Russell Sage.
Winsborough, H. H. and Peter Dickinson
1971   "Components of Negro-white income differences." Proceedings of the American Statistical Association, Social Statistics Section:6-8.
Yancey, William L., Eugene P. Ericksen, and Richard N. Juliani
1976   "Emergent ethnicity: a review and reformulation." American Sociological Review 41:391-402.

THE IDIOM OF RACE:
A CRITIQUE OF PRESENTISM

MICHAEL BANTON

Students of the social sciences are taught to recognize ethnocentrism as a form of bias. They are less frequently taught to recognize its partner, which might well be named "chronocentrism" but is coming to be known by its simpler designation of "presentism." This is the tendency to interpret other historical periods in terms of the concepts, values, and understanding of the present time.

The historical study of racial thought and attitudes has often been flawed by an unreflecting presentism. Earlier writers are held up to scorn without any adequate attempt to locate their understandings within the context of the knowledge available to their generation. Modern writers all too easily neglect the shifts in the meaning attributed to the word "race" (for a recent example of a serious study vulnerable to this criticism, see Horsman, 1976). This essay will contend that as new modes of explana-

Research in Race and Ethnic Relations, Volume 2, pages 21–42
Copyright © 1980 by JAI Press Inc.
All rights of reproduction in any form reserved.
ISBN: 0-89232-141-5

tion of human variation have arisen, so the word "race" has been used in new ways, but the old uses have often continued side by side with the new ones. "Race" and associated words suggesting commonality of descent or character were developed into popular modes of thought and expression in many European languages in the eighteenth century so that they constituted an idiom in which people related themselves to others and developed conceptions of their own attributes. In the nineteenth century this idiom was extended through the identification of race with nation (and *Volk*), and the rise of potent beliefs about national character. Where previously there had been an emphasis upon supposed innate differences between persons distant in social rank, the stress was shifted to differences between people of distinct nations. Political circumstances helped mold these changes but they cannot be fully appreciated without taking account of changes in scientific understanding.

Possibly the most notable feature of race as a concept is the way it has inveigled observers into assuming that the main issue is that of the nature of differences between populations, and that they should concentrate upon what "race" *is*, as if this would determine the one scientifically valid use for the word. Physical differences catch people's attention so readily that they are less quick to appreciate that the validity of "race" as a concept depends upon its value as an aid in explanation. From this standpoint, the main issue is the use of the word "race," both in rational argument and in more popular connections, for people use beliefs about race, nationality, ethnicity and class as resources when they cultivate beliefs about group identities.

The failure to allow for changes in the sense in which the word race has been used has important ocnsequences, for those who misunderstand the past of their society are likely to misunderstand the present, because people judge the present in the light of what they believe the past to have been. The past cannot be properly understood if changes in the significance of words are not allowed for. Historians and sociologists judge their predecessors, but will themselves be judged by a later generation because they are not standing outside history. Since the limitations of their knowledge will bemuse their successors, they should be charitable in assessing the limitations of their predecessors.

PHENOTYPICAL VARIATION

Confronted with others who looked so different, people must constantly have asked, "Why are they not like us?" If some exaggeration may be permitted in order to present the argument in its simplest form, it can be suggested that the educated Europeans in the middle of the eighteenth, the middle of the nineteenth, and the middle of the twentieth centuries would have offered different explanations of the reason why Europeans, Africans and Asians looked different. Moreover, these explanations of human variation would have corresponded (though not precisely) to the kinds of explanation acceptable in the biological science of their time. If "race" was used as a term in that explanation, then the significance attributed to the word would have been different in the three instances. In the eighteenth century it might have been said that Africans and Asians looked different because they were of different descent, and "race" might have been used to designate a line of descent, as in writing of "the race of Abraham." In the middle of the nineteenth century such explanations might well have been considered unsatisfactory and it might have been asserted that the outward differences between Africans and Asians were part of a more general pattern of variation in the mental abilities of groups and their suitability for living in particular regions of the world. In the wake of this mode of explanation "race" came to be used as a synonym for "type," which was on occasion defined as a primitive or original form independent of climatic or other physical influences. Types were thought to be permanent and the theory of racial typology left no room for the modes of explanation introduced by Darwin and Mendel.

The educated man addressing himself to these questions in the middle of the twentieth century would not have been satisfied with either of these explanations. He would, or should, have said that Africans and Asians looked different because they inherited different genes. In the African gene pool the genes determining such physical features as skin color were different because the process of natural selection had operated in favor of genes conferring an advantage in the environment in which people had to live. He would have explained that physical variation could not be accounted for by reference to a postulated range of pure types, but was the product of adaptation by selection and had to be studied statistically using the methods of population genetics. In this scheme of thought, the word race can be used as a synonym for subspecies, that is, a subdivision of a species which is distinctive because its members are isolated from other individuals belonging to the same species. Because of their isolation, its members mate with one another and so reproduce their distinctive features; but if, through migration, their isolation were reduced and they mated with others of the same species but not subspecies, their distinctiveness would disappear.

This essay seeks to explain the main variations in the use of the word "race" by relating them to these modes of explanation. It argues that throughout the three centuries "race" has been used both to designate categories of mankind and to explain certain of their characteristics, but the relation between designation and explanation has varied. When "race" has been used to identify a group of people of common descent it has often been a synonym for "nation"; it has served to identify a population but there has been little suggestion that by so identifying it, any special characteristics of the population have been explained. When "race" has been used with the implication that it designates a permanent zoological type, its claim to explanatory power has been much higher. When "race" has been used as meaning "subspecies," the implication has been that the individuals so designated have something in common biologically but that, without further investigation and more detailed argument, this explains relatively little about them.

Having reviewed the use of the word "race" in connection with these three modes of explanation, the essay will go on to discuss the possibility that the word is coming to be employed in a fourth sense that has little explanatory significance.

RACE AS DESCENT

When Greene's book, The Death of Adam (1959), asserts that Adam, as the first man of history, began to die in the minds of scholars about the time of Newton, the reference is not just to the declining acceptance of a biblical story but to a whole paradigm of explanation. It also dates the change a little earlier by referring to the beginning of the process and to the most advanced thinkers of the period. As Greene remarks, "before the seventeenth century no pressing need had been felt to group plants and animals into species, genera, orders, classes, and the like." John Ray, the pioneering natural historian of the late seventeenth century, declared, "... the number of true species in nature is fixed and limited and, as we may reasonably believe, constant and unchangeable from the first creation to the present day." The criterion of species was common descent, presumed or actually observed. "A species is never born from the seed of another species and reciprocally," he stated. This meant that regardless of differences, individuals belonged to the same species if their descent from the same ancestors could be proved or reasonably inferred.

Up to the eighteenth century at least, the dominant paradigm in Europe for explaining the differences between groups of people was provided by the Old Testament. It was the story of God's creating the world and, on the sixth day, of his making "Adam" (alternatively translated as "the man'') in his own image. The Old Testament provided a series of genealogies by which it seemed possible to trace the peopling of the world and the relations which different groups bore to one another. Thus Augustine derided the idea that there might be men in unknown lands on the other side of the world because the suggestion that some of Adam's descendants might have sailed there was "excessively absurd." Many writers attempted to ascertain the date when the world was created by working back through these genealogies. Others attempted to explain the assumed inferiority of black people by reference to a curse supposedly placed by Noah on the descendants of Ham, decreeing that they should be servants of his sons Shem and Japheth; or by relating it to the dispersal of peoples after the fall of the tower of Babel. Implicit in such arguments is the assumption that differences are to be explained by tracing them back to particular events the consequences of which are then transmitted genealogically. This is also a view of the world in which God is likely to intervene to punish or reward particular individuals and in which men are therefore less motivated to develop and improve classificatory concepts like that of species. As the quotation from John Ray indicates, a species was seen simply as the product of an arbitrary action by the Creator.

Within a paradigm of explanation in terms of descent there were several possible ways of accounting for physical variation. First, it could be held that differences of color and such like were all part of God's design for the universe; perhaps, as in the hypothesis about the curse on Ham's descendants, they were the result of divine judgment; perhaps, though, they were a part of God's plan that had not yet been revealed or that man could not properly understand, and this led to a line of reasoning which may be called racial romanticism. Secondly, it could be held that physical differences were related in some way to climate and environment and were irrelevant to the important questions of man's obligations to do God's will. Thirdly, it was sometimes argued that since the differences between Europeans, Africans and Asians were repeated in successive generations they must have had separate ancestors. It was hazardous and perhaps unnecessary to challenge the story of Adam directly, so the doubters suggested that the Old Testament account was incomplete: Adam was the ancestor of the Europeans alone. The debate about whether mankind consisted of one or many stocks had to be cast in terms of the dominant paradigm and therefore it was phrased as a choice between monogenesis and polygenesis.

The use of ''race'' as a term in explanations of this kind is reflected in the first major definition of the word given in the *Oxford English Dictio-*

nary (1910), viz.: "I. A group of persons, animals, or plants, connected by common descent or origin." This is the principal sense in which the word is used in English in the sixteenth, seventeenth and eighteenth centuries, and it continues to be used, though rather less frequently, in this sense. But already in the sixteenth century the notion of likeness because of descent was generalized and "race" was used to denote instances of likeness without any claim of common descent, like Dunbar's reference in 1508 to "backbiters of sundry races" and Sidney's of 1580 to "the race of good men." As the Dictionary records, this use continued into the nineteenth century, as with Lamb's reference to "the two races of men": the men who borrow and the men who lend, but thereafter it was less frequent.

If there was a principle explaining the differences in the appearance of peoples, either theistic or atheistic, then it could have operated through either moral or physical causes. Moral causes would today be called cultural: they consisted of the ways in which men responded to their environment. Physical causes were inherited dispositions and capacities. Both monogenists and polygenists used the word "race" to designate the outwardly identifiable populations of their time, but the same word meant different things to them. The monogenists believed that men started off the same and had become different because of climate and their different response to environmental opportunities. The polygenists suspected that men must have been different to begin with and their understanding of race was later systematized as "type."

For an illustration of how people subscribing to these two schools of thought could use the same word in what superficially appears to be the same sense, but draws upon two different modes of explanation, it is appropriate to turn to an essay by the historian Macaulay on the capacities of Negroes. It was written in response to a report by a Major Moody, who contended that though blacks in the West Indies could work hard, their preference for leisure was such that they would not do so unless coerced. According to Macaulay's reading, Moody maintained that there was an instinctive and unconquerable aversion between the white and black races which stemmed from a physical cause. Against this, Macaulay contended that the blacks did not work harder because, unless they emigrated, they could not get an adequate return for their labor. The antagonism, he said, was caused by slavery and for the Major to prove his case he needed to provide evidence of the alleged aversion in circumstances unaffected by slavery or the memory of it. Both men used the word "race" to designate blacks and whites: "the two races could not live together," wrote

Moody, while his critic referred to the "policy which excludes strangers, of all races, from the interior of China and Japan. Where Moody stressed "the consequences arising from physical differences in form, colour, feature and smell," Macaulay referred to "the Gypsey race, one of the most beautiful and intelligent on face of the earth . . . persecuted under a thousand pretexts . . . yet the remnant of a race still preserves its peculiar language and manners" (Macaulay, 1827: 137–38, 151–52). It should be noted that Macaulay, who elsewhere displayed his own variety of ethnocentrism, misrepresented his opponent's arguments (Williams, 1978), but yet it is still clear that for the one writer the history of a race was determined by its physical nature; for the other, its history was the story of how more varied circumstances caused it to become or remain distinctive.

RACE AS TYPE

Classification by descent was more easily manageable so long as the number of species was fairly limited, but with the revival of observation and the exploration of new continents in early modern times, the number of known kinds of plants increased rapidly. It was time for someone to distinguish essential forms from accidental variations, and to define a stable unit on which botanical classification could be based. The problem was most pressing in botany, but in principle it applied to all biology. The man who did most to resolve it was the Swedish naturalist known to later generations as Linnaeus (1707–1778).

In Linnaeus' view, natural history consisted of describing the various productions of the earth, their appearance, their habits, their relations to each other, and their uses. Implicit in this conception of classification as the goal of science was the belief that nature had been constructed on a pattern discoverable, at least in part, by human reason. It was man's duty to study nature diligently so that he could come closer to God, could better understand His purposes, and could glorify Him in his works. At the heart of the conception of nature to which Linnaeus came was the idea of an *oeconomia,* a rationally ordered system of means and ends. The earth, with its delightful variety of climate and topography, was populated with an equally varied assemblage of living beings, each perfectly adapted to the region in which it lived. The economy of nature lay in the balance between its constituent elements. Linnaeus never tired of describing the mechanisms which maintained the adaptation of organism and environment and the equilibrium of species (Greene, 1959: 134–37). God had created not a series of individual species but a self-regulating system. He did not need to intervene in the day-to-day affairs of his creation. The man who more than anyone else extended the method of Linnaeus to the study of the animal kingdom and—though only in outline—to that of man, was the French comparative anatomist Cuvier (1769-1832). The system which he hoped to discover by relating animal structure to conditions of existence was the "great catalogue in which all created beings have suitable names, may be recognized by distinctive characters, and are] arranged in divisions and sub-divisions." Cuvier's method of classification rested heavily upon the conception of a type (defined by the Oxford English Dictionary as "a person or thing that represents the characteristic qualities of a class; a representative specimen"). If the right representative specimen was chosen, then the essential of the category could be understood. Cuvier divided man into three main subspecies (which he called races): Caucasian, Mongolian, and Ethiopian, which were further subdivided. He stated that they were all one species but they had been separated by some great natural catastrophe. He presented the three races as differing permanently in ability because of the biological differences between them that were as yet little understood. Thus the earlier physical cause interpretation of human variation was given a new foundation.

Cuvier's influence was immense, and during the course of the nineteenth century the notion of type was extended to the analysis of poetry, aesthetics, biography, personality, culture, social movements, and many kinds of differences other than those of interest to biologists. His teaching was one of the principal factors behind the emergence in the middle years of the nineteenth century of an international school of anthropological thought. It is important to note that the conception of type was independent of the Linnaean classificatory system. A zoological type could be a genus, a species, or a subspecies. Critics therefore protested that the notion of type was redundant since the Linnaean classifications would serve. As the usual criterion for a species was that its members could breed with one another, and since the races of man engaged so frequently in interbreeding, *Homo sapiens* must be one species. The typologists criticized the orthodox definition of species. Prominent among them were Charles Hamilton Smith, Samuel George Morton, Joseph Arthur de Gobineau, Robert Knox, Josiah Clark Nott, George Robbins Gliddon, James Hunt, and Karl Vogt. They are often identified as proponents of "scientific racism" but their key concept was that of the permanence of types and their theory is better designated as "racial typology." Though there were variations from one writer to another and

Vogt at least changed his opinions significantly, they more or less agreed in presenting man as a genus divided into types which in effect were species. They believed that each type was permanent and was suited to a particular zoological province of the earth's surface, but they recognized that the actual races of the contemporary world were all mixed. They accounted for this by arguing that hybrids were ultimately sterile so that though because of human foolishness, races might deviate from their type, nature kept the deviation within bounds. An alternative interpretation was advanced by Gobineau who believed that the mixing had gone much too far and had spoiled the stocks responsible for progress so that humanity was going into decline (see Banton 1977:32–55).

The typological mode of explanation differed from the previous one in being agnostic about origins. The typologists rejected earlier beliefs that the earth was about six thousand years old. Whatever might have happened in earlier epochs, within the period for which there was anatomical evidence types appeared to have been constant. One of the main attractions of typology was that it offered a theory of history purporting to explain the differential pattern of human progress. The record of history also contributed to the theory by revealing the special cultural attributes of types that went along with the physical differences. Since changes were the outcome of the essential characteristics of types in relation to particular environments, the theory attributed little significance to purely contingent events like the reported curse upon Ham's descendants. Though the typological theory could be reconciled with a belief in polygenesis it was really of a very different kind. For its appeal it relied on the one hand upon science rather than the Bible, and on the other, upon the growing European acceptance of an association between differences in physical appearance and ability to build a progressive civilization.

Some of these writers, like Smith, Nott, Gliddon, and Broca, made a clear distinction between "type" and "race." Gobineau, Knox and Hunt utilized the distinction but were less careful, and Knox indeed usually used "race" where on his own terms "type" would have been preferable. In the subsequent period a few writers did try to keep to the expression "type" but it is noticeable that in the very considerable literature about the nature of racial differences published in the United States after the Civil War there is a strong tendency to use the word "race" in the sense of "type." It is unfortunate that the major study on American writing in this period—apart from its strong inclination to presentism— regards race and type as synonymous. It does indeed quote a passage in which Nott refers to the "permanence of races, types, species, or permanent varieties, call them what you please" (Haller, 1971: 80) but when

Nott, in *Types of Mankind* (1854: 95) wrote, "every race, at the present time, is more or less mixed," he was clearly referring to actual physically distinguishable populations and not to permanent types. Many of the passages in Haller's book (e.g., the reference in the American context to "both races," 1971: 208) refer to the latter usage and the interpretation of them is less clear than it would be were the distinction drawn. It would probably be worthwhile engaging in further more detailed research into the usage of the authors of the period in the light of Mayr's analysis (1972) of the multiple nature of the reorientation necessitated by Darwin's discovery of natural selection.

It could also be of interest to trace the ways in which the European idiom was carried to other continents. In South Africa before World War I, any reference to the races was likely to relate to the English-speaking and the Afrikaans-speaking sections of the white population. Equally, it was common to refer to the Zulu race, the Xhosa race, the Tswana race, differentiating groups within the African section of the population. Before World War II it seems to have been unusual to employ "race" to distinguish blacks from whites. Field Marshal Smuts wrote of the European type and the African type, identifying ethnic groups within these types as races (Graaff, 1973: 4). Most writers were less meticulous but it is interesting to note that the Memorandum of Association marking the foundation in 1929 of the South African Institute of Race Relations sets out as the main objective the encouragement of "co-operation between the various sections and races of the population of South Africa" as if blacks and whites constituted sections that were divided into races (Horrell, 1976).

A similar terminology was transported to Canada. In his 1839 *Report on the Affairs of British North America,* Lord Durham declared, "I found a struggle, not of principles but of races." He wrote continually of the two races and entitled one section of his report "The Gulf between the Races." But it is equally important to note that he presented each of these two races as the product of its history and institutions, and could refer to "the books . . . by which the minds of the respective races are formed." What he called a struggle of races he also described as "the fatal feud of origin," calling upon the eighteenth-century sense of race rather than upon typology. Later the French- and English-speaking populations came to be designated Canada's "founding races." French Canadians as well as those of English origin were content to identify themselves racially but there seems to have been little occasion to group the two races as divisions of a European type opposed to the Eskimo or North American Indian types.

In the twentieth century there has been a strong criticism of the use of racial doctrines to justify the inferior position or treatment of groups identifiable by physical characteristics. This leads contemporary students to look for assumptions about race whenever such groups are disparaged. It is therefore relevant to remark that whenever distinctive groups are brought together in unequal relations there is a tendency for people on either side to speak of ''them'' and ''us'' and to attribute to ''them'' all sorts of disvalued characteristics. It is possible to argue that members of the other group are feckless or inferior without making any reference to race, or if the word is used, by employing it to designate a group without implying that its members' characteristics have thereby been explained. James Walvin's documentary history of the Negro in England collects a variety of extracts from writings of the sixteenth to nineteenth centuries in which the authors speculate about the origins of differences between blacks and whites, speak for and against the slave trade, and dispute about the industry of blacks in the West Indies. Hardly any of them use the word ''race.'' Even Thomas Carlyle, in his notorious ''An Occasional Discourse on the Nigger Question'' in 1849, neither uses it nor attempts to explain why Negroes are as incapable as he maintains.[1] In the later eighteenth and early nineteenth centuries, especially in the United States, there were plenty of statements asserting the present inferiority of blacks, but the assertions did not necessarily claim that the differences were permanent. They tended to be particular statements, related to the speaker's experience. The political significance of the doctrine of typology was that it lifted such statements onto a plane of greater generality and offered an explanation. To assert that blacks were inferior might convince some people, but to say that blacks were one racial type out of a limited range and that the same principles which explained the whole range of phenomena also explained the particular characteristics of blacks was to advance a thesis of much greater intellectual pretension.

It was noted in the previous section that the explanation of human differences by reference to descent was associated with a concern about the original creation and God's design for the world. One outcome of this was the conclusion that God had created men of different colors for a purpose, and that each color category had its part to play in his plan. The most striking illustration of this approach to race is found in the early nineteenth-century school of thought rather misleadingly called *naturphilosophie* (see Banton, 1977: 35–40). An echo of it can be heard in the New England writer Ralph Waldo Emerson who in 1844 was insisting that the civility of no race could be perfect so long as another race was degraded, for mankind was one. Yet within a decade Emerson had been attracted to Knox's explanations and was arguing that England's economic prowess was the result of "the rare coincidence of a good race and a good place" (Nicoloff, 1961: 124, 139). It is difficult to be certain but it looks as if here, in less than a decade, Emerson switched from a sense of race as descent to that of race as type. It is also relevant that he did so in a book that tried to analyze the character of the Englishman. In later years there was to be a minor literary industry producing volumes about national character, and it was rooted in the presuppositions of racial typology.

RACE AS SUBSPECIES

Darwin cut the ground from under the feet of the typologists by demonstrating that there were no permanent forms in nature. Each species was adapted to its environment by natural selection, so that people of one racial type who migrated to a new habitat would there undergo change. The ups and downs of history could therefore not be explained in terms of the qualities of particular types. In the *Origin of the Species* Darwin recognized "geographical races or sub-species" as local forms completely fixed and isolated, but concluded that since they did not differ from each other in important characteristics there was no certain way of deciding whether they should be considered species or varieties. He employed the word race primarily when referring to domestic races as the outcome of human breeding, and presented them as incipient species, for as his subtitle suggested, it was by natural selection that favored races became species (Darwin, 1859: 62–63, 73).

Darwin's revolution was so complex (Mayr, 1972) that it took decades even for the specialists to appreciate its implications. In the 1930s, more than seventy years after the publication of the *Origin of Species*, new lines of reasoning and research in biology led to the establishment of population genetics. Human variation was to be comprehended statistically in terms of the frequencies of given genes within the gene pool of the relevant population. This meant that for biologists, "population" was the successor concept to the discredited notion of racial type, and race could be legitimately used only as a synonym for subspecies, as explained above.

Yet the first adaptations of Darwinian thought to social affairs preserved much of the older mode of explanation, in part because the reorientation demanded of people was so great, and in part because of the particular circumstances of the late nineteenth century. That period saw unparalled technological advances which helped knit together the peoples of Europe in larger, more effective units, and to increase the gap between them and the peoples of most other regions. Social evolution was pictured therefore not as adaptation to changing environments but as the story of man's progress to superior modes of living. Sociologists represented it as a process in which men first lived in small bands, then successively as members of clans, tribes, peoples, states and empires. Groups designated as races were often thought to belong somewhere in such a scale; skin color and similar traits served as signs of membership in groups that had progressed in different measure, and therefore functioned as boundary markers. The conception of race as subspecies is not easily grasped by the man in the street, whereas that of race as type is much simpler and can easily be twisted to deal with conflicting evidence. The idea of race in the popular mind in the twentieth century has therefore usually been that of race as type. This conception was invalidated by Darwin's work, whereas that of race as descent was not. Although confusing, it is therefore still legitimate to use the word ''race'' in the earlier sense.

RACE IN CURRENT USAGE

The idea of race was important to Europeans in the late nineteenth century on account of its value in philosophies of history. It was widely believed that the success of the European powers sprang from the qualities inherent in the white race, or races, and that these promised continuing European supremacy. Probably there would be less support for such views in Europe and North America in the 1970s. The bulk of the population is more likely to believe that the ups and downs of nations in history are a reflection of technological skill and material resources, though this is not a question that has been thought worth detailed investigation. Probably more people would agree that the cultural characteristics of racial groups are an outcome of environment and opportunity than would consider them genetically determined. Those who believe that the universe was built by divine design and that everything in it has a place in that design might well echo the racial romanticism of an earlier era. One twentieth-century

expression of this, though scarcely contemporary, is to be found in a
history of the British and Foreign Bible Society (Canton, 1924), entitled
The Five Colours. After the title page comes the verse:

> Not for one race nor one colour alone
> Was He flesh of your flesh and bone of your bone!
> Not for you only - for all men He died.
>   'Five were the colours', The Angel said,
>   'Yellow and black, white, brown and red;
>   Five were the wounds from which he bled,
>   On the Rock of Jerusalem crucified.
>
> —"The Vision of Peter"

If race remains a word in popular usage, religious groups concerned for
international harmony may well stress the complementarity of races and
again employ metaphors of this kind.

In England in the years preceding and following World War II, the
tendency was for less use to be made of the idiom of race. Sir Julian
Huxley and A. C. Haddon, the senior anthropologist at Cambridge, set
the tone in *We Europeans,* in which they declared that ''the term race as
applied to human groups should be dropped from the vocabulary of science'' because it had ''lost any sharpness of meaning'' (1935: 107). Ideal
types had to be distinguished from the existing mixed populations which
might also be political and cultural units and were best called ethnic
groups. The utility of race as a concept in either biological or social
science was doubted by the leading authorities in both fields, while the
extravagancies of Nazi rhetoric, coupled with the growing threats presented by their regime, helped to discredit it in popular usage. Earlier
practices, such as that of identifying the French- and English-speaking
sections of the Canadian population as ''the two races'' began to appear
quaint. The same could be said of Sir Winston Churchill's rather archaic
usage in his *History,* of which Book I was entitled ''The Island Race.'' In
1957 he could still write about the early twentieth century, ''meanwhile in
Europe the mighty strength of the Teutonic race, hitherto baffled by
division or cramped in lingering mediaeval systems, began to assert itself
with volcanic energy'' (1958: Preface). This echo of a previous century's
parlance was a reminder of the change that had been occurring.

From the scientific standpoint it is unfortunate that just as the word
''race'' was being less used in any context where it might be thought to
claim explanatory value, New Commonwealth immigration into England
led to its greatly increased use in the press and in popular speech to

designate the different population groups. An examination of the present use of the words "race," "races," and "racial" would probably show that they are employed chiefly to designate outwardly identifiable categories, and that people differ greatly in the degree to which they believe or assume that the labels explain anything. If questioned about why such groups should be called races, or what is the nature of race, many people will say that they are not sure but leave such matters to the experts. Since there are few situations in everyday life which require a precise use of "race" its employment in a diverse and loose fashion causes few problems.

Two situations calling for precise definition of ethnic or racial identification are provided by censuses and legislation. In the United States after World War II social scientists moved away from the use of race to designate social categories, preferring to write about minorities. The Federal government has been more slow to change: until recently they were using five "racial/ethnic categories," viz.:

1. *American Indian or Alaskan Native:* A person having origins in any of the original peoples of North America.
2. *Asian or Pacific Islander:* A person having origins in any of the original peoples of the Far East, Southeast Asia, or the Pacific Islands. This area includes, for example, China, Japan, Korea, the Philippine Islands, and Samoa.
3. *Black/Negro:* A person having origins in any of the black racial groups of Africa.
4. *Caucasian/White:* A person having origins in any of the original peoples of Europe, North Africa, the Middle East, or the Indian subcontinent.
5. *Hispanic:* A person of Mexican, Puerto Rican, Cuban, Central or South American, or other Spanish culture or origin, regardless of race.

This list is quoted from the Federal Interagency Committee on Education Report, vol. 2(1), May 1975.]
The Association of Indians in America—i.e. of Indians from Asia—protested against their classification as whites. In May 1977 the President's Office issued a revision of Circular A-46. It modified category 1 by adding the qualification "and who maintains cultural identification through tribal affiliation or community recognition." To the first sentence of category 2 it added "the Indian subcontinent." Category 3 was redesignated "Black." The numbers of categories 4 and 5 were changed

round; 5 is now designated simply "White," and the reference to the Indian subcontinent has been deleted. The circular further states that if separate race and ethnic categories are used, the minimum designations are:

a. Race:
   • American Indian or Alaskan Native
   • Asian or Pacific Islander
   • Black
   • White
b. Ethnicity
   • Hispanic origin
   • Not of Hispanic origin.

Thus "ethnicity" becomes a subdivision of the categories Black and White alone. The circular also lays down that when someone is "of mixed racial and/or ethnic origins" the category to be used is that which "most closely reflects the individual's recognition in his community." The designation "non-white" is no longer acceptable.

In Britain there is currently a controversy about categories to be used in the 1981 census. It is said that the procedure almost certain to be recommended by the Office of Population Censuses and Surveys contains the instruction: "*Race or ethnic group* (1) Please tick the appropriate box to show the race or ethnic group to which the person belongs or from which the person is descended. 1. White; 2. West Indian; 3. African; 4. Arab; 5. Turkish; 6. Chinese; 7. Indian; 8. Pakistani; 9. Bangladeshi; 10. Sri Lankan; 11. Other" (Mack, 1978).[2] It will be unfortuante if the word "race" is retained in this context by the American and British governments since this will add legitimacy to the lingering remains of the typological doctrine that were on their way to the lumber room of discarded science. The United States government's use of ethnicity as a subdivision of a racial category has little support in contemporary social science, but their practice of classifying individuals by their having origins in particular peoples seems far preferable to the British assumption that a person can belong to a race. It should also be noted that though the British Race Relations Act of 1976 penalizes discrimination on racial grounds, it does not define race, and that there is at present little case law that bears upon this question. The Act does, in Section 3 (i) define racial groups but only as "a group of persons defined by reference to colour, race, nationality or ethnic or national origins."

Consideration of these issues does, however, suggest that a fourth use of the word "race" is now being established. It is an administrative and political use which does not pretend to any explanatory significance but will doubtless be used to support old-style racial explanations. The political implications of the racial idiom have always been complex. It can be argued, for example, that a salient feature of the use some Englishmen made of it in the middle and later decades of the nineteenth century was to celebrate the positive qualities of their own stock and that the disparagement of the qualities of other stocks was to start with only an incidental consequence of their self-centeredness. (Sir Charles Dilke's *Greater Britain* of 1868 is an illustration of this.) Only as contact and conflict between Europeans and non-Europeans became closer did the political use of racial doctrines become important. In recent times peoples who have been the victims of such doctrines have been inclined to turn the tables by appealing for nonwhite solidarity against whites. In the United States some blacks prefer to identify themselves in racial terms because they believe that their experience of disadvantage has been so much more profound that that of white ethnic minorities. In the United Kingdom it seems as if people who stand to the left in political terms are the more inclined to identify New Commonwealth immigrant minorities in racial terms because they wish to challenge the typological preconceptions which seem still to be widespread in the white population. This appears to have been the major reason why the agency established under the 1976 Act has been called The Commission for Racial Equality whereas its predecessor was the Community Relations Commission. Therefore though it may seem desirable on strictly academic grounds to abandon the use of the word race, there are political pressures, from nonwhites as well as whites, from radicals as well as conservatives, which are likely to keep it in current use and to shape the fourth stage in the career of this troublesome concept.

OTHER PERSPECTIVES

If the meaning of the word race has changed in the way suggested, reflecting changes in popular understanding of the significance of phenotypical variation, then it is reasonable to expect that the character of the arguments which get classified as "racist" will have changed likewise. When race meant descent, then it may be expected that whites considered alliance with blacks as socially dishonorable. When race meant type, whites would have seen sexual union with blacks as producing a stock physically inferior to whites but superior to blacks. When race meant subspecies, most members of the public would not have comprehended the workings of inheritance and selection, and since it takes time for scientific advances to reach the wider public it might be expected that the typological doctrine would have retained its appeal.[3] Now that race is coming to be defined by bureaucratic and political concerns it is not surprising that there is no agreement upon a clear definition of racism.

Historical evidence is not lacking to support this thesis at least in respect to the change between the first and second stages. In 1771 the Viceroy of Brazil ordered the degradation of an Amerindian chief who, "disregarding the signal honours which he had received from the Crown, had sunk so low as to marry a Negress, staining his blood with this alliance" (Boxer, 1963: 121). Such a statement recalls a judgment that in eighteenth-century Latin America the "almost pathological interest in genealogy" and honorable descent was characteristic of the age (Mörner, 1967: 59). It suggests that it is the social rather than the physical consequences of marriages between persons of contrasting status which are to be avoided, and can be placed alongside the French *memoire du roi* of 1777 that declared of the transplanted Africans in Saint Dominique:

> Whatever distance they may be from their origin, they always keep the stain of slavery, and are declared incapable of all public functions. Even gentlemen who descend in any degree from a woman of color cannot enjoy the prerogatives of nobility. This law is harsh, but wise and necessary. In a country where there are fifteen slaves to one white, one cannot put too much distance between the two species. . . (Hall, 1972: 183–84).

This is an explicitly political argument which utilizes a doctrine of descent—to which Europeans admitted exceptions when it suited them—in order to exclude a category of people from civil rights. It lacks the biological presupposition which a twentieth-century reader might expect.

Literature in English does not suggest so clear a distinction between justifications of inequality rooted in ideas of descent and of racial type. Suggestions that interracial mating would contaminate the blood and result in degradation can often be found before the nineteenth century. This may be in part because belief in descent as a principle of social organization had been so much weakened in English political conceptions and was contradicted by the democratic ideals of white Americans. Physical cause explanations of phenotypical variation seem to come earlier in the English writing and there are condemnations of interracial mating where in other cultures the criticism is directed more toward interracial marriage. Other circumstances may therefore contribute in some measure to the difference. But in more recent times, English-language writing does show a tendency for those opposed to integration to base their arguments upon cultural rather than biological differences (Banton, 1970: 28–32). This can be seen as providing some confirmation of the expectation that as the use of race in the sense of type has lost scientific legitimacy, so the nature of "racism" was likely to change.

Another opportunity for checking the argument of this essay might be provided by a comparison of the synonyms for race in different European languages, for if changes in scholarly understanding of physical variation led to changes in vocabulary, this should have been experienced in languages other than English. There may well have been a shift in German from the use of words like *Menschheitstämme* to *Geschlecht* and then *Menschenrasse* which would reflect the change in scientific thought toward typology. Guizot's dictionary of French synonyms of 1822 compares race with *lignée, famille,* and *maison* as different designations of relationships among people of the same blood: *parenté* indicates the same fathers and mothers; *race* indicates origin; *lignée,* a line of children and grandchildren; *famille,* those who are brought up together; *maison* is used in the English sense of "royal house"; there is no discussion of when it is appropriate to write *de race noble* in place of *de sang noble* or how *race* compared with *descendence.*[4] Superficial observation would suggest that with the rise of ethnic antagonism in Algeria twenty years ago, *race* was used more frequently, and in the sense of type. Detailed studies of any such shifts, and of any similar shifts in Spanish and Portuguese, might provide a broader foundation for studying the idiom of race as it has changed over time and in relation to political circumstances.

CONCLUSION

Physical differences between peoples have been observed throughout human history; all over the world people have developed words for delineating them. "Race" is a concept rooted in a particular culture and a particular period of history which brings with it suggestions about how these differences are to be explained. It lends itself to use in a variety of contexts and gets elaborated into a whole style or idiom of interpretation. In the earliest phase of its career "race" meant descent at a time when people understood little of the biology of descent. In the nineteenth century "race" became identified with a controversial scientific theory that was found to be erroneous and which, had science been a more logical and less human enterprise, should have been discarded after 1859. Instead, the old idea was salvaged and rebuilt on a foundation quite different from that of the pre-Darwinian era, while in the present it is being used for purely political purposes to identify communities without intending to imply that the chief differences between them stem from inheritance.

Some scholars overlook these differences in the meaning that has been given to the word; they interpret the racial attitudes of earlier centuries in terms of their own generation's understanding of biological variation and condemn anything which to a modern reader smacks of racial intolerance. This practice diminishes some of the differences between periods of history; it distracts attention from the forces for change which exist in the present and will extend into the future. Presentism tends to slow down the process whereby erroneous or unhelpful formulations are discarded, and it can be pernicious when analyses of past events are distorted by a desire to support a contemporary political strategy. Since all writers will be influenced in some degree by the circumstances of their own time, and most believe that it is possible to learn lessons from history, the problem is implicit in any account of another period, but it can still be kept under control. Since people's ideas about the special characteristics of their own time are influenced by their beliefs about previous periods they have a particular reason to be on their guard against presentism.

NOTES

1. The great exception is the egregious historian of Jamaica, Edmund Long, who in 1774 presented Negroes as a distinct species just above orangutans in the great chain of being, but Long *is* an exception.

2. In March 1980 it was announced that the 1981 United Kingdom census would not contain any question on race or ethnic origin. See also White, 1979.

3. Although overlain by some other lines of thought, sophisticated writers for a time advanced social Darwinist theses that racial prejudice served an evolutionary function, while the slogan 'survival of the fittest' seemed to justify white aggressiveness overseas.

4. The author is obliged to Professor Michael Biddiss and Mr. M. J. O'Regan for helping with these comparisons.

REFERENCES

Banton, Michael
  1970   "The concept of racism." Pp. 17–34 in Sami Zubaida (ed.) Race and Racialism. London: Tavistock.
  1977   The Idea of Race. London: Tavistock.
Boxer, C. R.

1963   Race Relations in the Portuguese Colonial Empire, 1415-1825. Oxford: Clarendon Press.
Canton, William
1925   The Five Colours. London: The Bible House.
Churchill, Winston S.
1956-1958   A History of the English-speaking Peoples. London: Cassell.
Darwin, Charles
1959   On the Origin of Species by Means of Selection; or, The Preservation of Favoured Races in the Struggle for Life (Page references to New York: Mentor Books edition).
Graaff, J. F. de V.
1973   "Kosmos and Chaos: The racial attitudes of Jan Christian Smuts." Unpublished MSc. thesis, University of Bristol.
Greene, John C.
1959   The Death of Adam. New York: Mentor Books.
Hall, Gwendolyn Midlo
1972   "Saint Domingue." Pp. 172-192 in David W. Cohen and Jack P. Greene (eds.), Neither Slave nor Free: The Freedmen of African Descent in the Slave Societies of the New World. Baltimore: Johns Hopkins University Press.
Haller, John S.
1971   Outcasts from Evolution: scientific attitudes of racial inferiority 1859-1900. Urbana: University of Illinois Press.
Horrell, Muriel
1976   Personal communication.
Horsman, Reginald
1976   "Origins of racial Anglo-Saxonism in Great Britain before 1850." Journal of the History of Ideas 37: 387-410.
Huxley, Julian S. and Haddon, A. C.
1935   We Europeans: A Survey of 'Racial' Problems. London: Cape.
Macaulay, Thomas B.
1827   "The social and industrial capacities of Negroes." Reprinted in *Race,* 1971, 13: 133-164.
Mack, Joanna
1978   "A question of race." New Society 43, 5 Jan: 8-9.
Mayr, Ernst
1972   "The nature of the Darwinian revolution." Science, 176: 981-989.
Mörner, Magnus
1967   Race Mixture in the History of Latin America. Boston: Little, Brown.
Nott, J. C. and Gliddon, Geo. R.
1854   Types of Mankind: or, Ethnological Researches Philadelphia: Lippincott.
Nicoloff, Philip L.
1961   Emerson on Race and History: an examination of "English Traits." New York: Columbia University Press.
Wagley, Charles
1959   "The concept of social race in the Americas." Actas del XXXIII Congress International de Americanistas. San Jose, Costa Rica, I: 403-417, reprinted in Wagley, The Latin American Tradition. New York: Columbia University Press, 1968, 55-174.

Walvin, James
   1971   The Black Presence: A Documentary History of the Negro in England, 1555–
           1860. London: Orbach and Chambers.
White, R. M.
   1979   What's in a name? problems in official and legal usages of "race". New Com-
           munity, 7: 333–349.
Williams, David O.
   1978   "Macaulay and the commission to Tortola." Unpublished MSc. thesis, Univer-
           sity of Bristol.

BLACK SUICIDE AND THE RELATIONAL SYSTEM:
THEORETICAL AND EMPIRICAL IMPLICATIONS OF COMMUNAL AND FAMILIAL TIES

ROBERT DAVIS

In recent years suicide among Blacks in the United States has received increasing attention among behavioral scientists specializing in suicide research. Generally these specialists disagree with one another about the etiological factors associated with Black suicide, but they all agree that suicide is increasing among Blacks, especially among young Blacks (see Seiden, 1972; Peck and Litman, 1973; Davis, 1975; Slater, 1973; Woodford, 1965). A review of previous literature on the phenomenon of Black suicide suggests a variety of factors that may be considered as determi-

Research in Race and Ethnic Relations, Volume 2, pages 43–71
Copyright © 1980 by JAI Press Inc.
All rights of reproduction in any form reserved.
ISBN: 0-89232-141-5

nants of the current increase in Black suicide, including such factors as migration, rage and frustration, selected urban stresses (i.e., unemployment, poverty, racism, etc.), movement into the American middle class, breakdown in traditional social institutions (i.e., church, family, school, etc.), and certain conditions associated with fatalism.

In addition, part of the increase is thought by some to be the artifact of reporting. As a result of being more cognizant of Blacks, coroners are thought to be investigating ambiguous Black deaths much more thoroughly today than they did in the past. Another possible explanation argues that the increase in Black suicide can, at least in part, be a result of suggestion and imitation once the initial reports of an increase appear in the news media. Phillips (1974) has shown that this could be so.

In the present analysis I will be examining the possibility of a link between the loosening or weakening of communal and familial ties, indicators of what Henry and Short (1954) have called "Strength of the Relational System," and Black suicide. Evidence can readily be mounted to support such a view since social scientists assume that close social bonds are both critical to the individual and help integrate him/her into the social system. Furthermore, a lack of such bonds is frequently used in the deviance literature to explain a wide variety of deviant behaviors. In short, I examine here the effects of weakening of the relational system (i.e., alienation from traditional institutional structures, relationships and groups within the Black community) upon Black suicide while controlling for relevant social structural variables. I propose that such social relations are necessary for the development of positive and functional forms of response to recurrent stressful social situations.

RECENT TRENDS IN BLACK SUICIDE

Despite the common belief that suicide in the United States is a problem of whites, recent research emphasizes the fact that it is democratically distributed (Hendin, 1969; Peck and Litman, 1973; Seiden, 1970, 1972; Davis, 1975). Most people, both white and Black, are surprised to learn that suicide is a serious problem among young Blacks. In recent years, the following observations have been made nationally concerning the high frequency of suicide among young Blacks:

1. The suicide rate of 15- to 19-year old nonwhite females has exceeded the toll for their white female age peers. (*Vital Statistics of the United States, 1965–1967*).

2. The suicide rate of Black males, ages 20–24, has approximated and at times surpassed that of their white male age cohorts (*Vital Statistics of the United States, 1965–1967*).
3. The suicide rate of nonwhite males and females, ages 15–34, is now higher than it has been in more than 50 years. Furthermore, during 1966 and 1967 the national suicide rate for nonwhite males, ages 25–29, surpassed the rate of their white age peers (*Vital Statistics of the United States, 1967–1969*).
4. Blacks between the ages of 15 and 24 commit suicide at a rate higher than that of the total Black population of all ages (Seiden, 1972).
5. Among Black Americans, suicide rates peak between ages 25 and 34 (Seiden, 1970).

Although the total death rate for suicide among whites exceeds the rate of Blacks (12.8 per 100,000 versus 6.0 per 100,000), the latest available mortality statistics (1970–1975) indicate that the pattern of youthful Black suicide is persisting and has become even more pronounced. The suicide rate for Blacks as a whole has increased by 22 percent; furthermore, within the youthful age ranges of 20–24 and 25–29, the increases were 16 and 36 percent, respectively. Most significant, however, is the fact that the bulk of Black suicides (47 percent) occur among young Blacks ages 20–34 (see Table 1).

Table 1. Recent Trends in Black Suicide by Selected Age Groups and Sex, 1970–1975.

Age and Sex	Number	Percentage		Average Annual Rate	Percentage Change 1970 to 1975
Males, all ages	6,142	75.5		9.3	25.9
20–24	1,206	14.8	36.1	22.3	15.1
25–29	999	12.3		23.6	41.6
30–34	728	9.0		20.1	9.1
Females, all ages	1,994	24.5		2.7	8.0
20–24	362	4.5	11.0	5.5	10.4
25–29	311	3.8		6.1	13.8
30–34	221	2.7		4.9	21.8
Both sexes, all ages	8,136	100.		5.8	21.6
20–24	1,568	19.3	47.1	13.0	16.2
25–29	1,310	16.1		14.0	35.8
30–34	949	11.7		11.7	1.7

Sources: Vital Statistics of the U.S., 1970–1975 (Volume 2—Mortality, Part A, Tables 1–26).
   U.S. Bureau of the Census (1975, pp. 23–28).

Whereas in the past the suicide rate among Blacks was considerably lower than among whites, in the most recent decade the suicide rate among young Blacks has risen to the point where it is nearly as high as that of their white age peers. Examining the 20–24 age group of both races throughout the United States for the six-year period, 1970–1975, we find suicide rates of 12.8 per 100,000 for Blacks and 14.2 per 100,000 for whites. Within the 25–29 age group, the Black suicide rate increased to 14.1 per 100,000 (the highest recorded rate for this age group to date) and the white suicide rate increased to 15 per 100,000. At age 35 and above, however, the suicide rate for Blacks remains relatively low (see Tables 2 and 3).

What emerges from these data and other contemporary studies of Black suicide is the striking contrast in age distribution: Whereas suicide among whites increases in direct relationship to advancing chronological age, suicide among Blacks reaches its peak in the youthful years. Older Blacks seldom take their own lives. Does this reflect the older Blacks' ways of coping—the old training that emphasized sustaining oneself in the face of overwhelming obstacles—and/or access to stable, positive social relations within the Black community?

To some extent, the youthful nature of Black suicide is reflective of a national increase in adolescent suicides across all racial groups (Peck, 1971). However, this increase is most pronounced among Blacks, and in recent years has reached epidemic proportions. On a national level, recent mortality statistics disclose that the Black suicide rate peaks 5 years earlier (20–34) than it did 7 years ago (25–34). In addition, the suicide rate of young Black males between ages 20 and 34 is the same as that of white males in the same age group. At ages 25–29, however, the suicide rate of Black males has surpassed that of their white male age cohorts. Scanning the data in Table 3, we can readily see that the average annual suicide rate for the 6-year period 1970–1975 for Black males ages 25–29 is 23.6 per 100,000, whereas the rate for their white male age cohort is 21.6 per 100,000. Furthermore, within this same age range, Blacks commit suicide at a rate of a little more than two times (14.1 per 100,000 vs. 6.0 per 100,000) greater than that of the total Black population of all ages.

Given these rates, it is feasible to assume that youthful suicide is a substantial problem within the Black community. It is seen as particularly acute because the Black community is being robbed of some 30 to 40 years of useful manpower, earned wages, sources of reproduction, and a host of other contributions that young people make to society.

Table 2. Suicide Rates, per 100,000 U.S. Population by Race, Age, and Sex, 1970 and 1975.

	BLACKS						WHITES					
	1970			1975			1970			1975		
All Ages	5.1	8.1	2.5	6.2	10.2	2.7	12.4	18.0	7.1	13.6	20.1	7.4
<5 yrs	—	—	—	—	—	—	—	—	—	—	—	—
5–9 yrs	—	—	—	—	—	—	—	—	—	—	—	—
10–14 yrs	0.4	0.3	0.4	0.2	0.2	0.3	0.7	1.1	0.3	0.9	1.4	0.4
15–19 yrs	3.8	4.8	2.9	3.9	6.4	1.6	6.2	9.4	2.9	8.1	13.0	3.1
20–24 yrs	11.7	20.5	4.8	13.6	23.6	5.3	12.3	19.3	5.7	16.9	26.3	6.9
25–29 yrs	12.0	19.7	5.8	16.3	27.9	6.6	14.1	19.8	8.6	16.6	25.1	8.0
30–34 yrs	11.8	19.7	5.5	12.0	21.5	4.3	14.7	20.0	9.5	16.7	23.5	10.0
35–39 yrs	8.7	14.5	4.0	9.9	17.3	4.0	16.9	21.9	12.2	17.0	22.8	11.4
40–44 yrs	7.1	11.4	3.5	9.0	15.2	3.8	19.1	24.6	13.8	19.9	26.1	13.9
45–49 yrs	9.2	15.9	3.5	7.9	13.7	2.9	20.6	28.2	13.5	21.4	29.1	14.0
50–54 yrs	7.3	11.3	3.9	6.0	10.4	5.3	21.9	30.9	13.5	21.6	30.2	13.6
55–59 yrs	6.9	12.9	1.7	7.2	11.7	3.3	23.5	34.9	13.1	21.9	32.0	12.7
60–64 yrs	4.7	7.7	2.2	6.5	9.8	3.8	22.5	35.0	11.5	20.7	32.3	10.6
65–69 yrs	5.9	9.7	2.7	5.1	8.5	2.5	21.9	37.4	9.4	20.9	35.0	9.6
70–74 yrs	4.7	7.0	3.0	9.3	16.0	3.9	22.7	40.4	9.7	21.2	37.6	9.3
75–79 yrs	2.7	4.5	1.4	8.8	18.1	1.9	21.4	42.2	7.3	22.3	44.9	7.8
80–84 yrs	8.2	16.6	2.3	3.1	6.6	0.8	20.0	45.8	5.8	19.4	50.3	4.7
85+	5.8	10.2	3.1	1.3	3.8	—	20.0	45.8	5.8	19.4	50.3	4.7

Source: Vital Statistics of the U.S., 1970–1975 (Volume 2—Mortality, Part A, Tables 1–26).

47

Table 3.   Sucide Rates, per 100,000 U.S. Population by Race and Sex, 1970-1975.

Year	Black			White			Nonwhite		
	Total	Male	Female	Total	Male	Female	Total	Male	Female
1970	5.1	8.1	2.5	12.4	18.0	7.1	5.6	8.5	2.9
1971	5.3	8.0	3.0	12.5	17.9	7.3	5.9	8.6	3.4
1972	6.1	9.6	2.9	12.8	18.5	7.3	6.6	10.3	3.3
1973	5.9	9.7	2.5	12.8	18.8	7.0	6.4	10.0	3.0
1974	6.0	9.9	2.6	13.0	19.2	7.1	6.5	10.2	3.0
1975	6.2	10.2	2.7	13.6	20.1	7.4	6.8	10.6	3.3
Average Annual Rate	5.8	9.3	2.7	12.8	18.7	7.2	6.5	10.1	3.2
	Age Specific Suicide Rates								
	Ages 20-24								
1970	11.7	20.5	4.8	12.3	19.3	5.7	12.0	19.4	5.5
1971	11.6	17.8	6.6	12.5	19.0	6.2	12.1	17.8	7.1
1972	15.4	25.6	6.8	13.5	20.5	6.6	16.6	26.0	8.2
1973	13.5	24.1	4.8	14.9	24.3	5.5	14.1	23.3	5.8
1974	12.1	21.3	4.6	15.5	24.5	6.4	12.8	21.3	5.0
1975	13.6	23.6	5.3	16.9	26.3	6.9	14.4	23.6	6.0
Average Annual Rate	13.0	22.3	5.5	14.2	22.4	6.3	13.5	22.3	5.9
	Ages 25-29								
1970	12.0	19.7	5.8	14.1	19.8	8.6	12.6	20.1	6.0
1971	11.2	17.6	6.0	14.2	20.1	8.3	12.1	18.3	6.8
1972	14.2	23.1	6.8	14.9	21.0	8.8	14.4	23.1	6.9
1973	15.3	26.4	6.1	15.0	22.1	8.0	15.2	25.8	6.2
1974	14.3	25.0	5.3	16.1	23.8	8.4	14.2	24.0	5.9
1975	16.3	27.9	6.6	16.1	25.1	8.0	16.4	27.6	6.8
Average Annual Rate	14.0	23.6	6.1	15.0	21.6	8.4	14.3	23.6	6.5
	Ages 30-34								
1970	11.8	19.7	5.5	14.7	20.0	9.5	11.9	19.4	5.6
1971	10.9	17.0	6.1	13.9	18.5	9.5	11.3	16.7	6.6
1972	10.9	19.2	4.1	15.3	20.7	9.9	10.7	18.4	4.2
1973	10.8	19.2	3.9	15.2	21.4	9.1	11.1	18.9	4.4
1974	13.7	23.4	5.6	15.9	22.8	9.0	13.6	21.5	6.8
1975	12.0	21.5	4.3	16.7	23.5	10.0	12.9	20.9	6.0
Average Annual Rate	11.7	20.1	4.9	15.3	21.0	9.5	11.6	19.2	5.8

Soruce: Vital Statistics of the U.S., 1970-1975 (Volume 2—Mortality, Part B, Tables 7-6).

Suicide Among Black Women

Though nationally, death by suicide for Black females is reportedly on the increase (see Maris, 1969; Slater, 1973; Seiden, 1972), it is worthy of note that the ratio of Black male to Black female suicide is 3.4 to 1 for the total Black population of all ages, and 4 to 1 for the peak age range of 20-34 (see Table 3). It is interesting and somewhat puzzling that Black male suicide, which has not received the public attention of Black female suicide, occurs with such frequency during the 6-year period of this study. Considering the recent attention focused upon Black female suicide (Wylie, 1974; Reingold, 1974; Christian, 1973; Slater, 1973; Peck and Litman, 1973; Seiden, 1972), one would expect the current statistics to reflect suicide as a ''growing menace to Black women.'' However, the degree to which the suicide rate of young Black women has increased relative to the increase among young Black men suggests that suicide is indeed a menace, but primarily to young adult Black males in their twenties.

Of the 8,136 Black suicides occurring from 1970 through 1975, 1,944 (25 percent) were female, and 6,142 (75 percent) were male. During this same period, the corresponding rate of Black suicide per 100,000 Black population by sex was 2.7 and 9.3, respectively. Bear in mind that when we portion out the youthful age group (20–24), the Black male suicide rate is four times greater than that of the females. Even more astonishing is the fact that Black female suicide increased by only 8 percent from 1970 to 1975, whereas for Black males it increased by 25 percent (see Table 1). Generally the data indicate that although both sexes show increases from the earlier period, the increases are most dramatic among Black males for all age groups considered.

Within the 25–29 age group, Black male suicide increased by 42 percent as opposed to a 14 percent increase among Black female age peers. Similarly, within the 20–24 and 30–34 age groups, Black male suicide increased more rapidly than Black female suicide for the same age cohorts. More interesting is the fact that Black female suicide actually decreased by 22 percent within the latter age group. Furthermore, within the youthful Black age range 20–34, Black males account for 36 percent of all suicides, whereas Black females represent only 11 percent. It is among young Black males 25–29 that the highest average annual suicide rate occurs, 23.6 per 100,000; the corresponding Black female rate is 6.1 per 100,000. Hence, in this decade (1970s), the rate of suicide for young Black males is four times greater than that of young Black females.

When nonwhite data (Blacks comprised 94 to 90 percent of the total nonwhite population during these time periods) are analyzed for the time periods 1965–1969 and 1970–1975, we find that nonwhite male suicide increased more rapidly in every age group considered than did nonwhite female suicide (see Table 4). Most noticeable is the 59 percent increase within the 20–24 age group as opposed to a 34 percent increase among young nonwhite females. In the 30–34 age group, nonwhite female suicide decreased by 3 percent.

Table 4. Age Specific Nonwhite Suicide Rates by Sex for Selected Time Periods.

Age Group	1965–1969			1970–1975			Difference					
							1965–1969 and 1970–1975			Percentage of Change		
	Both Sexes	Male	Female	Both Sexes	Male	Female	Both Sexes	Male	Female	Both Sexes	Male	Female
All ages	5.0	7.7	2.5	6.5	10.1	3.2	1.5	2.4	0.7	30.0	31.2	28.0
20–24	9.0	14.0	4.4	13.5	22.3	5.9	4.5	8.3	1.5	50.0	59.2	34.1
25–29	10.9	17.1	5.6	14.3	23.6	6.5	3.4	6.5	0.9	31.2	38.0	16.1
30–34	10.9	16.8	6.0	11.6	19.2	5.8	0.7	2.4	-0.2	6.4	14.3	-3.3

Source: Vital Statistics of the U.S., 1965–1975 (Volume 2—Mortality, Part B, Table 7–6).

Finally, the present data fail to reflect suicide as occurring more often among 15 to 19-year-old Black females than their white female age peers. In fact, within this age group, we find average suicide rates of 1.7 per 100,000 for Black females as compared to 3.1 per 100,000 for white females. Even within the peak age range of 25–29, Black female suicide does not exceed the rate of its white age cohort (6.1 per 100,000 vs. 8.4 per 100,000).

Clearly, then, neither a "rapid" nor "dramatic" increase in the suicide rate of Black women is evident in the current data. Nor do the present data reflect a more rapid increase in the suicide rate among Black females relative to Black males. More important, this generalization is not altered when we focus attention upon the youthful age groups, i.e., ages 20–34.

Regional Distribution of Black Suicide

The total Black population of the United States was 24 million on April 1, 1974, representing an increase of 1.4 million over the April 1970 figure. The most recent estimate of the Black resident population was 24.4 million in April 1975 (U.S. Bureau of the Census, 1975). After declining steadily for the last three decades, the proportion of Blacks living in the South has leveled off at about 53 percent. Of the remaining 47 percent of the Black population, 38 percent reside in the North and 9 percent in the West (see Table 5).

Regionally, in 1970 the nonwhite suicide rate was highest in the West (8.9 per 100,000), and lowest in the South (4.4 per 100,000), with the North falling in between (5.4 per 100,000). The white suicide rate reflects a slightly different regional distribution for 1970 data. The highest rate, 17.7 per 100,000, occurs in the West (18 percent of white population), and the lowest rate, 10.3 per 100,000, in the North (53 percent of white population). The South, which accounts for 29 percent of the white population, has a rate of 13.1 per 100,000. For both races, the data reflect an inverse relationship between the proportion of the population residing in a region and its suicide rate (see Table 5).

For the 1975 data, the regional pattern is virtually identical to that of 1970, with the exception of noticeable increases for both races. In the South, which has the lowest nonwhite suicide rate (5.7 per 100,000), suicides increased by 30 percent among nonwhites. Conversely, the nonwhite suicide rate increased by 13 percent in the West, the region with the highest nonwhite rate (9.8 per 100,000). Finally, the nonwhite suicide rate increased by 26 percent in the North, where the nonwhite rate is 6.8 per 100,000.

Table 5.   Regional Distribution of Suicide per 100,000 U.S. Population by Color:
1970 and 1975, and Change from 1970 to 1975.

	South	North			West
		Northeast	North Central	Total	
1970					
Nonwhite	4.4	4.5	6.2	5.4	8.7
White	13.1	9.2	11.2	10.3	17.7
Total	11.3	8.7	10.7	9.8	16.8
1975					
Nonwhite	5.7	6.0	7.5	6.8	9.8
White	15.8	10.2	11.9	11.1	17.8
Total	13.9	9.8	11.5	10.7	16.9
Percentage Change					
1970–1975					
Nonwhite	29.5	33.3	21.0	25.9	12.6
White	6.1	8.2	10.5	7.7	0.6
Total	23.0	12.6	7.5	9.2	0.6
Percentage Distribution					
of U.S. Population					
Black	53.0	19.0	20.0	39.0	9.0
White	29.0	24.0	29.0	53.0	18.0

Source: Vital Statistics of the U.S., 1970–1975 (Volume 2—Mortality, Part B, Table 7-6). U. S. Bureau of the Census (1974, Table 3).

According to 1975 data on whites, the suicide rate increased by less than 1 percent in the West, the region with the highest white suicide rate (17.8 per 100,000). The North, which has the lowest white suicide rate (11.1 per 100,000), recorded an 8 percent increase from 1970 to 1975. Similarly, the white suicide rate increased by 6 percent in the South, where the white suicide rate is 15.8 per 100,000.

The only other observation worthy of note in Table 5 is that suicide rates are increasing more rapidly among nonwhites than whites across all regions of the United States. Furthermore, among nonwhites the greatest increase occurs in the North, particularly the Northeast (33 percent), and the South. Hence, it appears that those regions with low nonwhite rates are experiencing the greatest increase in suicide. Finally, in addition to the inverse relationship noted earlier, there exists an inverse relationship between the percentage change from 1970 to 1975 and the suicide rate for both races across each region.

Table 6 presents nonwhite suicide rates for the 17 states with the largest Black population for 1970 and 1975. The data presented here show that for both periods, California (9.9 and 9.7 per 100,000), Ohio (7.4 and 9.5

Table 6. Nonwhite Suicide Rates for States with the Largest Black Populations, by Sex: 1970, 1975, and Change from 1970 to 1975.

| States | Percentage Black Population | | | Suicide Rates | | | | | | Difference | | | | | |
| | 1960 | 1970 | 1975 | 1970 | | | 1975 | | | 1970–1975 | | | Percentage of Change | | |
				Total	Male	Female	Total	Male	Female	Total	Male	Female	Total	Male	Female
Mississippi	42.0	36.8	27.4	2.3	3.8	0.9	2.7	4.4	1.1	0.4	0.6	0.2	17.4	15.8	22.2
South Carolina	34.8	30.5	23.6	1.5	2.8	0.3	1.8	3.0	0.8	0.3	0.2	0.5	20.0	7.1	1.7
Louisiana	31.9	29.8	19.3	4.5	7.8	1.5	4.0	7.1	1.4	-0.5	0.7	-0.1	-11.1	8.9	-6.7
Alabama	30.0	26.2	27.4	2.9	4.2	1.6	2.2	4.3	0.3	-0.7	0.1	-1.3	-24.1	2.4	-81.3
Georgia	28.5	25.9	23.6	4.3	7.2	1.7	3.9	6.4	1.9	-0.4	-0.8	0.2	-9.3	-11.1	11.8
North Carolina	24.5	22.2	24.9	3.3	4.9	1.7	4.5	7.4	1.7	1.2	2.5	0.0	36.4	51.0	0.0
Virginia	20.6	18.5	16.5	5.5	8.3	2.6	3.0	4.5	1.6	-2.5	-3.8	-1.0	-45.5	-45.8	-38.5
Florida	17.8	15.3	14.8	4.7	6.2	3.2	4.4	7.4	1.5	-0.3	1.2	-1.7	-6.4	19.4	-53.1
Tennessee	16.5	15.3	11.6	5.7	9.4	2.3	4.7	7.7	2.2	-1.0	-1.7	-0.1	-17.5	-18.1	-4.3
Illinois	10.3	12.8	12.4	5.1	7.9	2.5	5.6	9.2	2.6	0.5	1.3	0.1	8.9	16.5	4.0
Texas	12.4	12.5	12.5	4.7	6.8	2.7	5.0	8.0	2.3	0.3	1.2	-0.4	6.4	17.6	-14.8
New York	8.4	11.9	11.3	3.6	5.9	1.5	5.0	8.1	2.5	1.4	2.2	1.0	38.9	37.3	66.7
New Jersey	8.5	11.3	11.2	3.5	5.4	1.8	4.5	7.4	2.0	1.0	2.0	0.2	28.6	37.0	11.1
Michigan	9.2	11.2	11.7	6.3	10.1	2.7	8.4	12.6	3.5	2.1	2.5	0.8	33.3	24.8	29.6
Ohio	8.1	9.1	9.5	7.4	11.0	3.9	9.5	15.4	4.4	2.1	4.4	0.5	28.4	40.0	12.8
Pennsylvania	7.5	8.6	8.9	7.3	11.4	3.5	9.8	15.6	4.9	2.5	4.2	1.4	34.3	36.8	40.0
California	5.6	7.0	7.7	9.9	12.0	7.8	9.7	12.9	6.7	-0.2	0.9	-1.1	-6.1	7.5	-14.1
District of Columbia	53.9	75.0	75.7	4.9	8.5	1.7	18.0	9.6	3.0	13.1	11.1	1.3	267.3	130.6	76.5

Source: Vital Statistics of the U.S., 1970–1975 (Volume 2—Mortality, Part B, Table 7-6).

53

per 100,000), Pennsylvania (7.3 and 9.8 per 100,000) and Michigan (6.3 and 8.4 per 100,000) recorded the highest nonwhite suicide rates. Correspondingly, Mississippi (2.3 and 2.7 per 100,000), Alabama (2.9 and 2.2 per 100,000), North Carolina (3.3 and 4.5 per 100,000), New Jersey (3.5 and 4.5 per 100,000), and New York (3.6 and 5.0 per 100,000) recorded the lowest nonwhite rates. Further inspection of Table 6 indicates that an inverse relationship between the percentage of Black population and the nonwhite suicide rate, which to a very large extent can be read as Black suicide rate, exists. This relationship is also supported by our regional data.

The most remarkable feature of Table 6, however, is that with the exception of Alabama, the states with the highest and lowest nonwhite suicide rates experienced similar net increases from 1970 to 1975. Furthermore, the greatest increases for both sexes occur in states ranked among those with the highest and lowest rates. Specifically, males experienced increases of 51 and 40 percent in North Carolina and Ohio, respectively; whereas female suicide rates increased by 67 percent in New York and 40 percent in Pennsylvania. Finally, it is worthy of note that in California, the state with the highest rates for both time periods, the nonwhite suicide rate decreased by 6 percent.

Table 7 presents Black suicide rates by sex for SMSA's with 50,000 or more Black population in 1970. The data indicate that 22 of the SMSA's have total rates of less than 10 per 100,000. Of these, the lowest rates are found in the Norfolk-Portsmouth, Virginia (3.1), Shreveport, Louisiana (3.7), and Mobile, Alabama (3.6) SMSA's. Special note should be given to the fact that each of the above SMSA's are located in the South. Of the remaining SMSA's, 13 have moderate rates (10 to 15 per 100,000 Black population), and 6 have rates greater than 15 per 100,000. The highest total suicide rates occur in the Los Angeles–Long Beach, California (21.4), Pittsburgh, Pennsylvania (21.5), Columbus, Ohio (18.4), Gary, Indiana (16.2), Cleveland, Ohio 16.0), and Louisville, Kentucky (15.5) SMSA's.

Among Black males half (51 percent;N = 21) of the SMSA's recorded rates greater than 15 per 100,000, with the Pittsburgh (41.3) and Columbus (31.5) SMSA's experiencing the highest rates. On the other hand, 90 percent (N = 37) of Black female rates occur in SMSA's with suicide rates of less than 10 per 100,000. The Los Angeles–Long Beach (18.3 per 100,000—the highest Black female suicide rate recorded to date), Charleston, South Carolina (11 per 100,000), and Richmond, Virgina (11.5 per 100,000) SMSA's recorded the highest female rates.

One, Greensboro-Winston-Salem-High Point, North Carolina, has a

Table 7. Black Suicide Rates per 100,000 Population,[a] for Selected SMSA's by Sex, 1970.

SMSA's	Both Sexes	Males	Females	Ratio of Males to Females
New York City	5.2	9.8	1.7	5.8
Newark, N.J.	8.0	11.3	5.4	2.1
Baltimore, Md.	10.9	17.7	5.2	3.4
Washington, D.C.-Md.-Va.	8.0	13.8	3.0	4.6
Memphis, Tenn.-Ariz.	7.6	11.8	4.5	2.0
Pittsburgh, Pa.	21.5	41.3	5.3	7.8
Cleveland, Ohio	16.0	25.6	8.4	3.1
Detroit, Mich.	11.6	18.3	5.8	3.2
Chicago, Ill.	8.8	15.2	3.6	4.2
St. Louis, Mo.-Ill.	6.1	12.0	1.7	7.1
Dallas, Tex.	7.3	9.6	5.3	1.8
New Orleans, La.	7.8	16.7	0.99	16.9
Houston, Tex.	6.8	10.8	3.4	3.2
Los Angeles, Cal. Long Beach, Cal.	21.4	25.3	18.3	1.4
San Francisco, Cal. Oakland, Cal.	14.1	22.3	6.7	3.3
Philadelphia, Pa.	9.8	15.3	5.4	2.8
Miami, Fla.	10.3	14.8	6.7	2.2
Atlanta, Ga.	14.0	24.6	5.8	4.2
Birmingham, Al.	8.6	12.8	5.5	2.3
Milwaukee, Wis.	11.1	11.6	10.6	1.1
Shreveport, La.	3.7	4.3	3.3	1.3
Mobile, Al.	3.6	3.7	3.6	1.0
Columbus, Ohio	18.4	31.5	3.9	8.1
Dayton, Ohio	10.8	12.0	9.9	1.2
Cincinnati, Ohio	9.9	15.1	5.8	2.6
Indianapolis, Ind.	11.6	17.1	7.0	2.4
Louisville, Ky.	15.5	32.2	3.0	10.7
Gary, Ind.	16.2	27.4	6.2	4.4
Kansas City, Kan.	12.6	18.0	8.3	2.2
Baton Rouge, La.	14.7	28.2	3.8	7.4
Jackson, Miss.	6.1	8.8	3.8	2.3
Nashville, Tenn.	13.2	25.0	3.1	8.1
Tampa-St. Petersburg, Fla.	13.4	22.1	6.1	3.6
Jacksonville, Fla.	8.6	10.1	7.5	1.3
Charleston, S.C.	8.0	4.4	11.0	0.4
Charlotte, N.C.	7.3	8.0	6.8	1.2
Greensboro-Winston-Salem-Highpoint, N.C.	7.0	15.8	0.0	0.0
Norfolk-Portsmouth, Va.	3.1	4.3	2.0	2.2
Richmond, Va.	14.0	17.1	11.5	1.5
Buffalo, N.Y.	4.7	6.7	3.0	2.2
Boston, Mass.	6.3	11.7	2.2	5.3
United States	5.1	8.1	2.5	3.2

Source: Computations by author from 1970 mortality tapes and 1970 county group public use sample.

[a] Since suicide is rare under age 18, all individuals below this age are excluded from the population of each SMSA. The rates, then, reflect suicides for individuals 18 and above.

[b] Only SMSA's with 50,000 or more Black population in 1970.

Black female suicide rate of zero (no suicide deaths occurred). Three others have extremely low rates (New Orleans, Louisiana, approximately 1 per 100,000; New York and St. Louis, Missouri, 1.7 per 100,000 Black female population.) The lowest rates among Black males, however, occur in the Mobile, Alabama, Shreveport, Louisiana, Norfolk-Portsmouth, Virginia, and Charlestown, South Carolina SMSA's. The respective rates are 3.7, 4.3, and 4.4 per 100,000 Black male population.

Finally, attention should be focused upon the last column of Table 7, in which the ratio of male to female suicide is recorded. The data clearly indicate that in the New Orleans SMSA there are 17 Black male suicides for every one Black female suicide. One other SMSA has a relatively large male to female ratio. Black males destroy themselves 11 times as frequently as their female peers in the Louisville, Kentucky SMSA.

These startling statistics indicate that the Black community is losing an increasing number of its future (youths) and its nurturing sources (women). Why is this particular segment of the Black population taking their lives?

It is the purpose of this paper to suggest a suitable explanation for the increasing suicide rate among young Blacks. Since this analysis draws heavily from materials presented elsewhere, the author makes no claim to originality for the theoretical ideas presented (see King, 1974; Holmes, 1974; Bohannan, 1960; Durkheim, 1951; Henry and Short, 1954; Maris, 1969; Breed, 1966).

THEORETICAL FRAMEWORK

Previous etiological explanations of Black suicide have been generally speculative, lacking research to substantiate their projections. This is due in part to the paucity of empirical studies specifically designed to evaluate substantive theories about the causes of Black suicide. In general, behavioral scientists, sociologists, and experts who deal with suicide all agree that prior to this decade Blacks have been characterized by a low, stable suicide rate. Black suicide rates have been analyzed in accord with the general theoretical proposition that they vary inversely with "external restraints," as indicated by such factors as low social status and the insulation that strong relational systems afford during periods of stress (Henry and Short, 1954; Maris, 1969; Breed, 1966). However, the prevalence of an increasing suicide rate among Blacks suggests either that the "external restraint theory" is not a suitable explanation of contemporary American black suicide or that restraints have weakened on the portion of the Black community that accounts for the increase (young Blacks). This study develops and analyzes the latter position.

Many observers point out that in the past, the stress of overt racism produced a kind of survival solidarity among Blacks that tended to reduce self-destructive behavior (Woodford, 1965; King, 1974). Recently, however, there has been an increase in social opportunities (more prestige, better jobs, higher education, etc.) and social status for some Blacks. Generally speaking, young Black males and females have experienced an uplifting of goals, aspirations, and expectations as a result of the perceived change toward greater opportunities within American society. Concurrently, this loosening of restraints has produced a false sense of freedom and security that has led to individualism and utilitarianism, which have tended to loosen or weaken the communal and family ties previously serving as a buffer against suicide.[1]

The theoretical propositions of Durkheim (1951) and research by Bohannan (1960) on African suicide document the importance of strong social ties. Durkheim's Law states that suicide varies inversely with the degree of integration of the group to which the individual belongs. When Blacks, due to excessive individualism, begin to internalize personal failures and frustrations, and no longer use the traditional structures, relationships, and groups within the Black community[2] to shield them from full personal impact, alienation and anomie set in, increasing the likelihood of self-destruction. Bohannan, in a cross-cultural study, also stresses the importance of group integration for suicide. He notes that the Dahomeans and Yaruba slaves in Brazil, well-integrated groups, tended to kill their masters, whereas the Fulani in Gabon and Mozambique, less well-integrated groups, tended to commit suicide. Generally, however, Bohannan observes that suicide rates in Africa are low because social ties are strong. Little or none of what Durkheim refers to as egoistic suicide, which arises from excessive individualism, exists.

Finally, it is worthy to note that Henry and Short (1954) advance the general proposition that suicide and the strength of the relational system are negatively related. My hypothesis, then, is that suicide among Blacks is likely to occur under conditions of weakened relations, i.e., loosening or weakening of communal and family ties. A theoretical model is presented in Figure 1. The primary interest of this model is the explanatory power of operational measures of weak social relations. As noted earlier, ''weakened relations'' refers to a process characterized by alienation from the traditional institutional structures, relationships, and groups within the Black community (i.e., churches, social clubs, fraternal organizations,

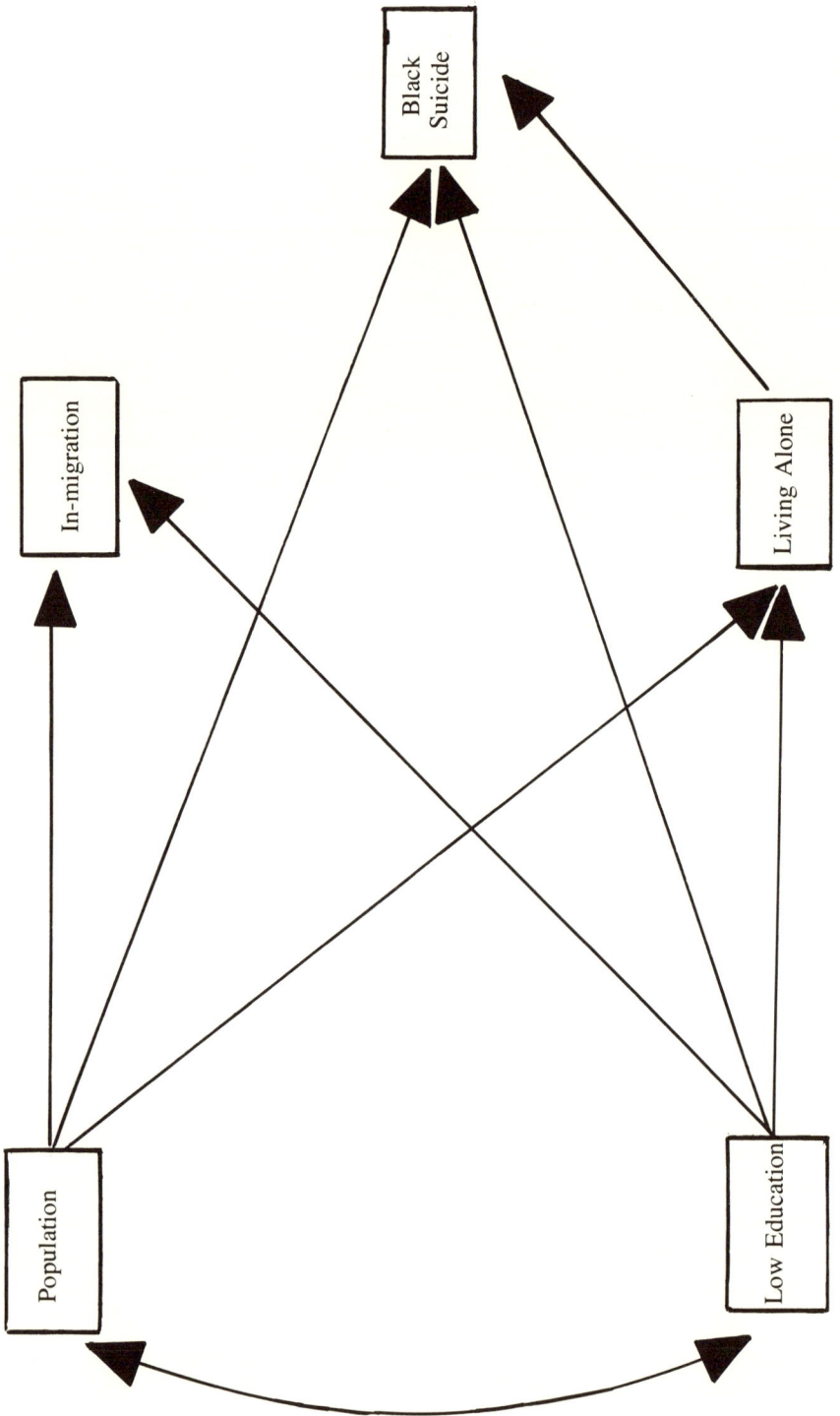

Figure 1. Determinants of Black Suicide

etc.). *Percent Black in-migrants,* defined as the percentage of Blacks 5 years old and over who moved into a state between 1965 and 1970, and *percent Black living alone,* defined as the percentage of a state's Black population living in a one-person household, are the operational measures employed.

The difficulties in dealing with new and unfamiliar urban stresses are poignantly presented by Breed (1966) in his examination of the consequences of urban migration for suicide among Blacks in New Orleans. Breed found that the suicides in his sample had higher than average inmigration rates; thus, we anticipate that in-migration will be positively related to suicide. But his study does not utilize any controls, and, by relying on only one city, he is unable to control for selective factors.

The literature on integration and isolation suggests that persons who live alone tend to lack close interpersonal ties (see Durkheim, 1951; Cavan, 1928; Schmid, 1928; Gibbs and Martin, 1964). In the case of suicidal behavior this means that there is typically no one to intervene to prevent suicide, for simple reasons of proximity if nothing else. Furthermore, if a person is integrated into a set of social networks his/her life takes on meaning and value. Percent Black living alone, as an independent measure of relative isolation (lack of integration), is also expected to be positively related to Black suicide.

Percent low education, defined as the percentage of a state's Black population with less than nine years of education, is utilized as an indicator of social class status.[3] The relationship between status and suicide has not been clearly established. Social class has been found to be related to suicide in all three directions: direct, inverse, and curvilinear (Henry and Short, 1954; Breed, 1966; Dublin, 1963; Gibbs, 1968; Maris, 1969; Powell, 1958; Rushing, 1968). It is quite possible that each of these relationships is equally valid because the association between social status and suicide may depend upon the particular population studied (see Maris, 1969:124) and the confounding relationship among different populations of strength of relational systems. The issue is not settled, however, and the present research is directed toward ascertaining a clear and careful examination of the relationship between Black suicide and social status.

Finally, *percent Black population 20–34* is controlled for, primarily because Black suicide is most pronounced within this age group. In the most recent decade, suicide among the youthful Black population ages 20–34 has risen to the point where it is nearly as high as that of their white peers (see Tables 1 and 2). Hence, we would expect this variable to be positively related to the Black suicide rate.

DATA AND METHODS

The data for this analysis are primarily taken from annual reports published by the National Center for Health Statistics (1970 and 1975), the United States Bureau of the Census (1970 volume), and the Current Population Survey (1971 and 1976). The data generated from these sources allow us to investigate the hypothesized relationship between weakened relations and Black suicide in states with the largest Black populations in 1970 and 1975. I have chosen to use two points in time to get some indication of the stability of the relationship over time.

My operational measures of Black suicide rely upon nonwhite suicide statistics. However, to a very large extent nonwhites can be read as Blacks, since census data reveal that Blacks comprise from 94 to 90 percent of the total nonwhite population between 1970 and 1975. In addition, by limiting this sample to only those states with the largest Black populations the probability of including Black suicides in our sample is increased.[4] In computing the suicide rates in 1970 and 1975 for each of the 17 states, the number of nonwhite deaths (numerator) was provided by the National Center for Health Statistics, and the estimates of the nonwhite population (denominator) were taken from the Current Population Survey (CPS). The independent and control variables were also drawn from the CPS. This large, highly professional and thoroughly routinized survey provides annual data on a whole host of social and economic variables. I also utilize the 1970 U.S. Census as the source of one of the independent variables.

Multiple regression analysis is used to determine the relative importance of each variable on Black suicide, while controlling for all other variables. Before turning to the substantive relationships, a word of caution is in order. This paper is concerned with an individual act and, to a large extent, with explaining it in terms of individual experiences, e.g., living in a one-person household. However, we are dealing with large aggregate units in this analysis; given the extreme rareness of the act in question and the characteristics of official statistics, an analysis such as this one virtually forces one to use large aggregate units. However, using such units imposes at least two serious limitations, one dealing with the strength and the other with the possible spuriousness of the observed relationships. These issues are dealt with briefly here; for those interested in an excellent discussion of the considerations involved in shifting levels of analysis, see Hannan (1971).

Assuming that a relationship between two variables exists at the individual level, using aggregate instead of individual data will typically increase the magnitude of the observed relationships. As a consequence, except under unusual conditions, one should not attribute the strength of a relationship found at the aggregate level to the individual level. Furthermore, a relationship that occurs at the aggregate level may, at least occasionally, not occur at the individual level. These characteristics of aggregate data, however, do not pose a serious problem to the present analysis, for I am primarily interested in (1) determining whether *any* relationship exists between the social relations variables and Black suicide after the relevant controls are introduced, and (2) assuming there is a relationship, obtaining a crude idea of the relative strength of this relationship vis-à-vis the traditional social structural variables, which are also aggregate measures. Finally, it is plausible that, across states, there could be a relationship between these measures of the relational system and Black suicides that does not exist at the individual level. Although such a relationship is mathematically possible, I am inclined to dismiss it as improbable.

THE ZERO-ORDER RELATIONSHIPS

Before assessing the overall results of the theoretical model, it is important to discuss the zero-order relationships between each independent variable and suicide. In Table 8, this information is presented for both time periods, 1970 and 1975. In most instances the correlations are *relatively* similar at the two points in time, although there are some exceptions to this general pattern. As noted earlier, emphasis in this model is on the explanatory power of two specific independent variables—percentage of Black in-migrants and the proportion of Black persons living alone—for Black suicide. Scanning the data in Table 8, we can readily see that the zero-order relationships between living alone and suicide are uniformly weak and positive for both time periods (r = .421 and .413). These coefficients indicate that, without utilizing any controls, states that have a high proportion of Black persons living alone also have a high suicide rate. Percentage of in-migration also tends to be positively associated with suicide; however, the coefficients are much stronger (r = .763 and .674). At both points in time, states with high percentages of Black in-migrants were more likely to experience high Black suicide rates. In sum, the data suggest, at the zero order level, that only one operational measure of the relational system (in-migration) is strongly related to the Black suicide rate.

Of the two control variables, low education has the strongest relationship with Black suicide. In the state data, we see that in 1970 and 1975, the measures of low education have relatively strong negative relationships (r = −.763 and −.795) with Black suicide. The proportion of the Black population 20–34, and low education show some change between with Black suicide in 1970 and a moderate positive relationship (r = .615) in 1975. The intercorrelations between inmigration, living alone, percent Black population 20–34, and low education show some change between the two time periods. In both time periods, the coefficients for the relationship between inmigration and low education are identical (r = −.813), indicating a strong negative correlation. However, this pattern is exceptional; the general pattern, as noted above, is one of *relative* similarity.

Table 9 presents the means for the two populations for all of the variables as well as percent Black, median income, and education. In 1975 there was a slightly larger proportion of the Black population between ages 20–34, a higher median income and median education, with a concomitant decline in low education and a slight decline in the percent Black population. The proportion of Blacks living alone and the suicide rate was higher in 1975, whereas inmigration was constant.[5]

Table 8. Zero Order Correlations Between Each Independent Variable and Suicide

	Suicide Rate	Percent In-migrant	Percent Living Alone	Percent Blk Pop. 20–34	Percent Low Education
Part A: 1970 (N = 17)					
Suicide Rate	1.000				
% In-migrants	.763	1.000			
% Living Alone	.421	.431	1.000		
% Black Pop. 20–34	.420	.549	.245	1.000	
% Low Education	−.730	−.813	−.593	−.771	1.000
Part B: 1975 (N = 17)					
Suicide Rate	1.000				
% In-migrants	.674	1.000			
% Living Alone	.413	.293	1.000		
% Black Pop. 20–34	.615	.513	.169	1.000	
% Low Education	−.795	−.813	−.231	−.729	1.000

Table 9.   Variable Means in 1970 and 1975.

	1970 (N = 17)	1975 (N = 17)
% Black In-migration	4.2	4.2
% Black Living Alone	7.2	8.7
% Black Pop. 20-34	19.4	21.8
% Black Low Education	35.8	31.0
% Black Population	17.9	16.1
Median Income	7,283	9,558
Median Years Education	9.36	9.78
Suicide Rate	4.6	5.2

Table 10 presents data that provide information needed to evaluate the variable linkages of the overall theoretical model diagrammed in Figure 1. In the first column coefficients of determination (r^2) are presented, indicating the amount of variation in suicide explained by each independent variable. In the second column standardized regression coefficients (Betas) are presented, indicating the relative importance of each variable, controlling for all other variables. In the third column multiple R^2's are

Table 10.   Regression Coefficients and Coefficients of Determination for the Dependent Variable Suicide Regressed on Four Independent Variables, 1970 and 1975.

Part A: 1970 (N = 17)

	r^2	Beta	Multiple Indep. R^2	Change in Multiple Indep. R^2
% In-migrants	.582	.7138[a]	.5921	.5921
% Living Alone	.177	.1132		
% Black Pop. 20-34	.176	.0014	.5921	.0000
% Low Education	.532	−.6951[a]	.6493	.0572
R^2		.649		

Part B: 1975 (N = 17)

	r^2	Beta	Multiple Indep. R^2	Change in Multiple Indep. R^2
% In-migrants	.454	.6052[a]	.5056	.5056
% Living Alone	.171	.2359		
% Black Pop. 20-34	.378	.3591	.6006	.0950
% Low Education	.632	−.6607[a]	.6908	.0902
R^2		.691		

[a] = significant at .05.

presented indicating the total amount of variation in the suicide rate explained by the variables considered. In the fourth column changes in the coefficient of determination produced by the addition of each variable to our baseline model are presented.

RELATIONAL SYSTEM

As indicated in the theoretical discussion, it was anticipated that the measures of the relational system would be related to Black suicide, and hypothesized that in-migration would be positively related to the Black suicide rate. The fact that there are such strong relationships for both time periods suggests that it is one of the most powerful predictors of Black suicide. In fact, the independent variance explained (r^2), and the Betas are the largest in 1970 and the second largest in 1975. However, for both time periods percent living alone is a weak predictor of Black suicide. This is surprising, given the attention directed toward this variable in the suicide literature (see Durkheim, 1951; Cavan, 1928; Schmid, 1928; Gibbs and Martin, 1964). At the zero-order level and with controls, we see that in both time periods living alone has a uniformly weak relationship to Black suicide. This set of variables (percent in-migrants and percent living alone) operating together account for approximately half of the "explained" variance in 1975, and nearly 60 percent in 1970. Thus, a link between a weakening of the relational system and Black suicide seems conceptually and empirically plausible, given the predictive power of our basic model.

As indicated in Table 8, at the zero order level we find that, in 1970, the percent Black population 20–34 has a weak positive correlation with the Black suicide rate; however, in 1975 this relationship is much stronger. With controls we see that in 1970 the relationship is virtually nonexistent, whereas in 1975 the relationship remains relatively weak and positive. In sum, the state data reflect a clear and consistent positive relationship (states with large Black populations ages 20–34 have higher suicide rates). However, the fact that we find such weak relationships suggests that the connection should be viewed with caution. Furthermore, percent Black population 20–34 adds absolutely nothing to the total explained variance in 1970, and accounts for approximately 10 percent of the total variances explained in 1975. In short, these data suggest that the proportion of the Black population 20–34 is not significantly associated with Black suicide in the 17 states considered in this investigation.

In both time periods, we find that low education has a relatively strong negative relationship with the Black suicide rate at the zero-order level and after controls are introduced. This variable, along with percent inmigrants, emerges as one of the most powerful predictors of Black suicide. In short, for these states, Black suicide is associated with high education and a high in-migration rate. The reasons for this pattern are not immediately obvious; and whether it reflects young, educated Blacks who are relatively mobile being particularly prone to suicide or whether there is a contextual effect is not clear. However, as shown by the last two columns of Table 5, when we add low education to the basic model, the total variance explained is 65 percent (6 percent increase) in 1970 and 69 percent (9 percent increase) in 1975.

REVISED MODEL

Given the weak predictive power of both living alone and percent Black population 20–34, it seemed plausible to determine how their deletion from the overall model would affect its ability to predict Black suicide. The data in Table 11 indicate slight increases in the standardized regression coefficients (Betas) for the remaining variables (percent in-migrants and percent low education) at both points in time. Specifically, the rela-

Table 11. Regression Coefficients and Coefficients of Determination for Revised Model: Suicide Regressed on In-migration and Low Education, 1970 and 1975

	r^2	Beta	Multiple Indep. R^2	Change in Multiple Indep. R^2
Part A: 1970 (N = 17)				
% In-migrants	.582	.7627[a]	.5817	.5817
% Low Education	.532	−.5808[a]	.6451	.0634
R^2		.645		
Part B: 1975 (N = 17)				
% In-migrants	.454	.6743[a]	.4547	.4547
% Low Education	.632	−.6431[a]	.6385	.1838
R^2		.639		

[a] = sigificant at .05.

tive importance of in-migration as a predictor of Black suicide increased by .0084 from 1970 to 1975. Similarly, percent low education increased in importance by .0623 for the same period. It is interesting to note that the direction of both variables remains the same in our revised model.

The most remarkable feature of Table 11, however, is the fact that the independent variance explained by percent in-migrants decreased by 13 percent in 1975. As expected (see note 5), in-migration is a more powerful predictor of Black suicide in 1970. Conversely, percent low education is more strongly related to Black suicide in 1975. The total variance explained by our revised model (64 percent) is increased by 18 percent in 1975 and only 6 percent in 1970. Finally, the model explains virtually the same amount of variance in both time periods.

DISCUSSION AND CONCLUSIONS

This paper suggested a number of reasons for expecting a weakening of social relations to be strongly related to the recent increase in Black suicide. Throughout the present analysis a great deal of concern has been focused upon the presumed detrimental consequences of becoming alienated from the traditional structures, relationships, and groups within the Black community. This form of alienation (i.e., excessive individualism) is thought to have its greatest effect among the youthful Black population (20–34), where the increase in suicide is most pronounced. I have been particularly concerned with the "isolating effect" of in-migration and living alone, which were designated as primary indicators of a weakening of social relations. These variables were hypothesized as limiting (in part or entirely) access to stable, positive functioning relations within the Black community, either at the family, group, communal, or institutional level.

An analysis of the variable relationships in the basic model shows only one of the "primary" variables to be a relatively strong and enduring predictor of Black suicide, particularly after controls are introduced. The fact that in-migration emerges as such a powerful predictor of Black suicide is consistent with the literature on Black suicide (e.g., Breed, 1966). The relationships with living alone were not striking. I have no explanation for the fact that previous literature on suicides (nonBlack) suggests theoretical reasons for believing that living alone would be related to Black suicide. Of all the variables considered, living alone is by far the one most weakly related to Black suicide (see Table 8). Although there are small relationships at the zero-order level, they virtually disappear when controls are introduced, indicating that living alone is, in fact, unrelated to the Black suicide rate.

A striking finding is that level of education, as measured by number of school years completed, is strongly related to Black suicide. Such a strong negative relationship (states with a low percentage of Blacks with less than nine years of education have high Black suicide rates) suggests that status is directly related to Black suicide. A comparison of the relationship associated with the above variables for 1970 and 1975 shows them to be relatively stable, particularly after controls are introduced. I would tentatively attribute some of this relationship to the empirical generalization that suicides are higher in the upper and middle classes[6] (see Henry and Short, 1954).

One of the most striking characteristics of Black suicide is that it is most pronounced in the youthful age group 20–34. The latest mortality data indicate that the pattern of youthful Black suicide is persisting, and that it has become even more pronounced in recent years (see Table 9). It was anticipated that the proportion of the Black population 20–34 would be related to Black suicides and the fact that such uniformly weak positive relationships were found, particularly after controls were introduced, suggests that this variable is not significantly associated with Black suicide.

In summary, the state data suggest that in-migration has a very strong effect on suicide, whereas living alone has, at most, a slight effect. Of the social structural variables considered, educational level appears to have had a major effect at both points in time, whereas the proportion of Black population ages 20–34 has virtually no effect in 1970 and a weak effect in 1975. Finally, we should note that in both the original and revised model, in-migration "explained" slightly more variance in the Black suicide rate in 1970 than it did in 1975. This probably should be taken as indicating that the isolating effect of being cut off from stable, positive social relations within the Black community has its greatest effect during the initial periods of settlement. Generally, however, the total variance "explained" by both models is identical for both time periods.

The data leave no doubt that improved social status (proxy-education) and isolation from protective social networks (proxy-migration) are strongly related to the recent increase in suicide among young (20–34) Blacks. Examination of recent research on the labor market position of young Blacks and a review of the established literature on the relationship between social mobility and isolation lends further support to this conclusion. Detailed investigation of the National Longitudinal Survey has found the occupational position of young Black men entering the job market after 1964 to be essentially the same as that of young whites with similar pre-market background characteristics (Hall and Kasten, 1973). The 1973 Occupational Change in a Generation Survey has shown marked advances in the relative position of Blacks, particularly those aged 25–34, compared to the 1962 comparable survey (Hauser and Featherman, 1975). Several studies oriented toward other labor market problems have found that the traditionally large negative impact of being Black on economic status has become much smaller than in the past (Wilson, 1978; Viscusi, 1976; Epstein, 1977; Astin, 1978). Hence, young talented, highly educated and skilled Blacks (primarily "prime-aged Black males" 20–44) were most likely to experience upward mobility via the social and economic progress of the sixties and early seventies. A fact that has probably not escaped the attentive reader, is that this prime-age range (20–44) corresponds to the age group in which the majority of Black suicides (mostly males) occur (20–34).

There is also an established body of literature that contends that social mobility results in isolation, or at least in the disruption of integration of primary and secondary group relations (cf. Durkheim, 1951; Sorokin, 1927; Janowitz, 1956; Blau, 1956; Litwak, 1960). The disruptive tendency of upward mobility for interpersonal relations received considerable attention from Blau (1956:290). He notes that:

> The upwardly mobile individual will have to give up old ties to gain status through association with higher-prestige groups and to avoid being identified with his former group. He may, however, find it difficult to establish extensive ties with individuals on the new level due to a reluctance on their part to accept him as an equal.

Hence, the Black community as a caring and protective system is likely to be less available to young upwardly mobile Blacks. When these young Blacks, because of racial differences, envy, personal crises, etc., begin to experience recurrent stressful social situations, they must do so without access to stable positive social networks within the Black community. Thus it seems plausible to conclude that the current increase in Black suicide can be attributed, at least in part, to young upwardly mobile Blacks who are isolated from their families, communities, and social institutions. The Black community, in effect, does not function as a protective society for these individuals.

NOTES

1. "False sense of freedom" refers to an illusion of widespread social opportunities and social acceptance within the dominant culture. "Individualism" and "utilitarianism" refer to the acceptance of white goals and values in the hope of social acceptance and individual profit or enjoyment. The American myth that "money means happiness" and automatic assimilation with the white culture is dominant.

2. I have in mind any organization, voluntary association or interest group which can be characterized as having a "community-recognized corporate identity." A variety of voluntary associations, from the local P.T.A. to the Urban League, have provided continuity and stability to the Black community's social structure. The participation of Blacks in political, religious and civil rights organizatons as well as fraternities, lodges, and the thousands of short-lived clubs and peer relations serves to provide Blacks an "opportunity for self-expression and status recognition." Similarly, these institutional community structures function to provide an avenue to compete for prestige, to be elected to office, to exercise power and control, and to win applause and acclaim. The important point is that these community structures provide members and leaders with prestige and social network systems that compensate for rejection, abuse, and the stresses and anxieties associated with suicide and depression.

3. This measure of status is not uncommon in sociological literature; however, median number of school years completed or the upgrading of our current measure to 12 years (high school grad) are alternatives to the procedure utilized.

4. The states included in this analysis are Mississippi, South Carolina, Louisiana, Alabama, Georgia, North Carolina, Virginia, Florida, Tennessee, Illinois, Texas, New York, New Jersey, Michigan, Ohio, Pennsylvania, and California.

5. For this paper, the data on in-migrants to each of the states is based on gross migration for counties for the 1965 to 1970 period. Hence, in the 1970 period there is a five-year lag, and in the 1975 period a ten-year lag. The assumption is that in-migration should have its greatest effect (if any) in the earlier period (initial period of settlement). In addition, gross migration data for 1970 to 1975 were not available to this researcher.

6. Henry and Short (1954) advance the proposition that suicide and status are positively related. They predict suicide will be highest among persons of high status and lowest among persons of low status.

REFERENCES

Astin, A.
1978   Four Critical Years. San Francisco: Jossey–Bass.
Banks, L. J.
1970   "Black suicide." Ebony 25:76–84.
Blau, P. M.
1956   "Social mobility and interpersonal relations." American Sociological Review 21:13–18.
Bohannan, P. (ed.)
1960   African Homicide and Suicide. Princeton, N.J.: Princeton University Press.
Breed, W.
1966   Suicide, migration, and race: a study of cases in New Orleans". The Journal of Social Issues 22:30–43.

Cavan, R. S.
1929   Suicide. New York: Russell and Russell.
Davis, R.
1975   "A statistical analysis of the current reported increase in the black suicide rate."
       Unpublished Dissertation, Washington State University, Pullman, Wash.
Dublin, L. I.
1963   Suicide: A sociological and statistical study. New York: The Ronald Press Co.
Durkheim, E.
1951   Suicide. Glencoe, Ill: Free Press
Epstein, W.
1977   "Schooling and occupation decisions." Doctoral dissertation, Harvard Univer-
       sity, Cambridge, Mass.
Gibbs, J. P. (ed.)
1968   Suicide. New York: Harper and Row.
Gibbs, J. P. and Martin, W. T.
1964   Status Integration and Suicide. Eugene, Oregon: The University of Oregon
       Press.
Hall, R. and Kasten, R.
1973   "The relative occupational success of Blacks and Whites." Brookings Papers
       on Economic Activity 3:781–798.
Hannan, Michael
1971   Aggregation and Disaggregation in Sociology. Lexington, Mass. Lexington
       Books
Hauser, R. M. and Featherman, D. L.
1975   "Racial inequalities and socioeconomic achievement in the U.S., 1962–1973."
       Institute for Research on Poverty, Discussion paper No. 275–75 Madison, Wis-
       consin: University of Wisconsin.
Henry, A. F. and Short, J. F. Jr.
1954   Suicide and Homicide. Glencoe, Ill. Free Press.
Holmes, C.
1974   "A study of black suicide." Dissertation Proposal.
Janowitz, M.
1956   "Some consequences of social mobility in the United States." Transactions of
       the Third World Congress of Sociology, 3–4:191–201.
King, L. M.
1974   "Suicide: a social analysis." Unpublished dissertation, University of
       California-Los Angeles, presented as paper at Drew Medical School Conference
       on Suicide, Los Angeles, Cal. April.
Litwak, E.
1960   "Occupational mobility and extended family cohesion." American Sociologi-
       cal Review 25:9–21.
Maris, R. W.
1969   Social Forces in Urban Suicide. Homewood, Ill.: Dorsey Press
Peck, M. L. and Litman, R. E.
1973   "Current trends in youthful suicides." Medical Tribune 14:11
Powell, E. H.
1958   Occupation, status and suicide." American Sociological Review 23:131–39.

Reingold, E.
  1974   Black suicide in San Francisco. Mini Consultation on Mental and Physical
         Health Problems of Black Women. Washington, D.C.: Black Women's Com-
         munity Development Foundation.
Rushing, W.
  1968   "Income, unemployment and suicide: an occupational study." Sociological
         Quarterly 9:493–503.
Schmid, C. F.
  1928   Suicides in Seattle, 1914 to 1925. Seattle: University of Washington Press.
Sorokin, P.
  1927   Social Mobility. New York: Harper.
Viscusi, W. K.
  1976   "Employment hazards: an investigation of market performance." Doctoral dis-
         sertation, Harvard University, Cambridge, Mass.
Vital Statistics of the U.S., Volume LL. Part A (Mortality), 1970–1975 Washington,
  D.C.: Government Printing Office.
Wilson, W. J.
  1978   The Declining Significance of Race. Chicago: The University of Chicago Press.
Woodford, J.
  1965   "Why Negro suicides are increasing." Ebony 20:89–100.
Wylie, F.
  1974   Suicide among black females. Mini Consultation on Mental and Physical Health
         Problems of Black Women. Washington, D.C.: Black Women's Community
         Deveolpment Foundation.

ADDITIONAL READING

Breed, W.
  1970   "The Negro and fatalistic suicide." Pacific Sociological Review 13:156–62.
Davis, R. and Short, J. F., Jr.
  1978   "Dimensions of black suicide: a theoretical model." Suicide and Life-
         Threatening Behavior 8:161–173.
Hendin, H.
  1969   Black Suicide. New York: Basic Books.
Phillips, D. P.
  1974   "The influence of suggestion on suicide: substantive and theoretical implica-
         tions of the Werther Effect." American Sociological Review 39:340–54.
Prudhomme, C.
  1938   "The problem of suicide in the American Negro." The Psychoanalytic Review
         25:187–204, 372–391.
Seiden, R. H.
  1972   "Why are suicides of young Blacks increasing?" Health Services and Mental
         Health Administration 87:3–8.
Seiden, R. H.
  1970   "We're driving young Blacks to suicide." Psychology Today 4:24–28.
Slater, J.
  1973   "Suicide; a growing menace to Black women." Ebony 33:153–160.

SOCIOLOGICAL, LEGAL AND POLITICAL ASPECTS OF THE SITUATION OF IMMIGRANTS IN SWITZERLAND

HANS-JOACHIM HOFFMANN-NOWOTNY

INTRODUCTION

As Stein Rokkan has rightly observed, Switzerland may be considered as a ''microcosm of Europe'' (1970: v). Her native population consists of four ethnic groups coninciding more or less with the four language groups.[1] In spite of this considerable number of minorities, political scientists believe Switzerland to have one of the most stable political systems of present times. Almond's hypothesis (1966: 259ff) that segmented democracies tend toward greater instability than homogeneous democracies has been refuted for Switzerland by Lijphart (1967), Lehmbruch (1967a, 1967b) and Steiner (1970).

Research in Race and Ethnic Relations, Volume 2, pages 73–95
Copyright © 1980 by JAI Press Inc.
All rights of reproduction in any form reserved.
ISBN: 0-89232-141-5

One of the reasons why Switzerland has succeeded in mitigating the problem of native ethnic minorities, finding acceptable compromises and thus maintaining a dynamic equilibrium probably consists in the fact that the ethnic separation line is only one among several other lines cutting across society in the vertical and horizontal directions. Some of the other lines concern religious affiliation, the development level of a region,[2] political affiliations, membership in one of the 26 highly autonomous cantons or of a certain social stratum.

All of these lines of separation do not tend to coincide with ethnicity; rather, they overlap in various ways, and the result is a large number of subcultures combining different characteristics.

While the problem of national ethnic minorities may be considered as solved or, rather, while these problems are being solved in a permanent political process, the same does not apply to the foreign national minorities that have been immigrating into Switzerland during the last 30 years. What has been said about the overlapping lines of separation within the national minorities does not apply to the foreigners; in particular, ethnic membership and membership in the lower class coincide for them.

In the first part of the present paper I will summarize briefly the quantitative dimensions of immigration, the number of immigrants, and their national and social composition. I will discuss also the problem of naturalization and the way Switzerland sees itself as a country of immigration. The latter is an important determinant of the legal and political

Table 1. Foreign Resident Population in Switzerland:[a] 1850–1978.

Year	Total Foreign	Percent of Total Population	Year	Total Foreign	Percent of Total Population
1850	71,970	3.0	1930	355,522	8.7
1860	114,983	4.6	1941	233,554	5.2
1870	150,907	5.7	1950	285,446	6.1
1880	211,035	7.4	1960	584,739	10.8
1888	229,650	7.9	1965	810,243[b]	13.8
1900	383,424	11.6	1970	982,887[b]	15.9
1910	552,011	14.7	1974	1,065,000[b]	16.8
1914	600,000	15.4	1975	1,012,710[b]	16.1
1920	355,522	8.7	1978	923,658[bc]	14.8

Source: Swiss Statistical Yearbooks and W. Bickel (1947: 159).
[a] The foreign "resident population" is made up of foreigners with a resident permit and foreigners with a permit to stay.
[b] Not included in these figures are functionaries of international organizations and members of their families.
[c] April 1978.

framework within which the problem of the immigrant minorities has to be treated.

The second part deals with the sociological background of the problem. Particular emphasis is put on the *Unterschichtung*[3] of the Swiss social and occupational structures and on the social and structural consequences of this phenomenon.

The third part deals with the legal position of the immigrants, which tends to differ from that of nationals although it is important to note the legal category to which the immigrant belongs. The fourth part discusses the political consequences of immigration. Since Switzerland is a plebiscitary democracy, immigration provokes specific reactions vis-à-vis the immigrant minority, which in turn specifically affects the legal and political arrangements made concerning the minority. In the final part I consider some aspects of the future development of the problem of foreign minorities in Switzerland.

QUANTITATIVE DIMENSIONS OF MIGRATION INTO SWITZERLAND

Historically, immigration into Switzerland is a recent phenomenon. As late as the eighteenth-century emigration out of Switzerland prevailed. During that century between 340,00 and 390,00 persons emigrated and most of them enlisted in foreign military services. While immigration into Switzerland started around 1850 the migratory balance only became positive during 1888–1900, showing a surplus of 74,000 persons. This fact must be kept in mind when examining the first table.

Already in 1914 Switzerland's share of foreigners was 15.4 percent, only slightly less than in 1974 (16.8 percent) when the peak of immigration after the Second World War was reached, and slightly more than in 1978 (14.8 percent). The decline in the number of foreigners in Switzerland that has occurred since 1974 has to be seen as a consequence of world-wide economic recession. As revealed by the ups and downs in the share of foreigners, caused by the two world wars and the world economic crisis of the 1930s, immigration was strongly dependent on external factors and was not constant.

Until recently, Switzerland recruited most of its foreigners from neighboring countries—Germany, France, Italy and Austria. In 1860 these four countries accounted for 97.3 percent of the foreign share, in 1910 for 95.2 percent and in 1960 for 87.1 percent. Since 1960 this share has decreased to 75 percent in 1970 and to 70 percent in 1977.

Table 2 shows, however, that there have been strong variations in the relative share of each of these four countries. The relative shares of the German and French immigrants have steadily decreased in favor of the Italian immigrants; this reduction happened first in the share of the French, later in the share of the Germans.

This change in the ethnic composition of immigrants was accompanied by a change in their social composition. Table 3 shows that while most immigrants always were workers—at least since statistics have been available—their share has greatly increased since 1941. Indeed, today we can speak of an immigration of workers. It must be added, moreover, that the ethnic change within the worker category has resulted in a strong increase in the share of unskilled and semiskilled workers.

This situation is intensified by the fact that there are an additional 110,000 workers in Switzerland employed on a seasonal basis, most of them unskilled or semiskilled (so-called saisonniers, before the recession set in their numbers amounted to more than 200,000). Basically, their stay is limited to nine months a year, but sometimes they work the whole year round. In view of this it seems to be justifiable to identify the problem of foreign minorities in Switzerland with the problem of foreign *workers*.

If one considers the share of the foreign resident population alone, all the tables presented thus far seem to prove that Switzerland is indeed an immigration country. But as implied earlier, that conclusion would not be entirely accurate. This becomes obvious when the number of naturalizations is related to the number of immigrants living in Switzerland.

As Table 4 shows, naturalization has been handled in a very restrictive way.[5] The rapid decrease in the share of foreigners (at least in a statistical sense) by way of naturalization, as was the case in the ''classic'' immigration countries, has never occurred in Switzerland. In 1969 the Swiss government stated again that naturalization should not serve as a ''decisive means'' toward reducing the proportion of foreigners: ''The number of naturalizations will and must continue to be small'' (Bericht des Bundesrates, 1969:22).

On the other hand, governmental policy is oriented toward maintaining and stabilizing the present share of foreigners, although it would definitely encourage remigration if the economic recession should continue. The rotation of immigrants, very high until the middle of the sixties, seems to be rapidly decreasing.[6] If in the future, immigration policy should indeed be handled in the same restrictive way as in the past; and if the number of foreign immigrants should be stabilized on the present

Table 2. Foreign Population Resident in Switzerland, by Nationality, 1960–1977.

COUNTRY	1860	1870	1880	1890	1900	1910	1920	1930	1941	1950	1960	1970	1975	1977
Germany	47,792	57,245	95,262	112,342	168,451	219,530	149,833	134,561	78,274	55,437	93,406	115,564	109,452	102,184
	41.6%	37.9%	45.1%	48.9%	43.9%	39.7%	37.2%	37.9%	35.0%	19.4%	16.0%	11.8%	10.8%	11.0%
France	46,534	62,228	53,653	53,627	58,522	63,695	57,196	37,303	24,396	27,470	31,328	51,396	51,885	50,601
	40.5	41.2	25.4	23.4	15.3	11.5	14.2	10.5	10.9	9.6	5.4	5.2	5.1	5.4
Italy	13,828	18,072	41,530	41,881	117,050	202,809	134,628	127,093	96,018	140,280	346,223	526,579	520,657	462,891
	12.0	12.0	19.7	18.2	30.5	36.7	33.5	35.8	43.0	49.1	59.2	53.6	51.4	49.6
Austria	3,654	6,232	13,309	14,181	24,413	40,058	21,680	20,095	—	22,153	37,762	43,143	41,504	38,431
	3.2	4.1	6.3	6.2	6.4	7.3	5.4	5.7	—	7.8	6.5	4.4	4.1	4.1
Other European	12,670	5,213	5,659	6,084	11,250	21,355	34,805	31,344	17,487	26,018	43,375			
	2.3	3.5	2.7	2.7	2.9	3.9	8.7	8.8	7.8	9.1	7.4			
Other Non-European	505	1,916	1,622	1,535	3,729	4,564	4,243	5,126	7,379	14,088	32,645			
	0.4	1.3	0.8	0.7	1.0	0.8	1.1	1.4	3.3	4.9	5.			
Spain												102,341	112,996	98,271
												10.4	11.2	10.5
Greece												9,029	10,205	9,168
												0.9	1.0	1.0
Yugoslavia												22,972	34,347	36,209
												2.3	3.4	3.9
Turkey												12,137	26,093	27,267
												1.2	2.6	2.9
Other												99,726	105,571	60,950
												10.2	10.4	11.6
Total	114,983	150,907	211,035	229,650	383,424	552,011	402,385	355,522	223,554	285,446	584,739	982,887	1012,710	932,743

78

Table 3. Foreign Work Force According to Occupation: 1900–1970.

Year	Self-employed	Directors	Leading technical employees	Other leading employees	Lower technical employees	Other lower employees	Skilled, semiskilled, and unskilled workers	Other	%
1900	16.5	←————————— 9.6 —————————→					69.7	4.2	100.0
1910	19.2	←—— 1.62 ——→		←————— 9.4 —————→			65.3	4.5	100.0
1920	19.8	0.3	0.3	1.3	1.5	9.4	63.1	1.2	100.0
1930	17.0	0.2	0.4	1.5	1.9	8.8	65.6	4.8	100.0
1941	21.4	0.3	0.3	1.8	2.1	10.2	60.3	3.5	100.0
1950	10.8	0.3	0.5	1.6	1.7	9.3	73.1	2.8	100.0
1960	3.3	0.4	←—— 1.5 ——→		2.6	6.7	83.7	1.2	100.0
1970	2.3	0.4	1.0	1.1	←—— 16.8 ——→		77.8	1.2	100.0

Source: Federal censuses.

Table 4. Regular Naturalization of Foreigners: 1900–1977.

	Year											
	1900	1910	1920	1930	1941	1950	1960	1965	1970	1975	1977	
Number naturalized	2,727	3,659	3,870	3,335	3,362	2,669	1,939	4,217	5,331	7,414	10,776	
As percent of foreign population	0.71	0.66	0.96	0.94	1.50	0.94	0.33	0.29	0.54	0.73	1.20	

Source: Swiss Statistical Yearbooks, various years.

level, then about 15 percent of the population, not being citizens, will be excluded from exerting those civil rights that are linked to the status of a citizen. It must be noted, moreover, that a considerable part of the foreign resident population has already been born in Switzerland.

THE SOCIOLOGICAL BACKGROUND OF A SOCIAL AND POLITICAL PROBLEM[7]

From a societal point of view international migration giving rise to problems such as the existence of foreign minorities in Switzerland is the consequence of exploitation of development lags in the international system. The fact that such development lags exist and that members of national societies are increasingly becoming conscious of them gives rise to two main directions of migrations: (1) migration in the direction of decreasing development leading to an *Ueberschichtung* of the immigration society; and (2) migration in the direction of increasing development, relevant for our discussion, leading to the *Unterschichtung* of the immigration country. *Unterschichtung* means that most immigrants occupy the lowest positions available in the social and occupational structures of the immigration country where they form a new social stratum at the very bottom of the stratified structure. Thus, the immigrants combine ethnic characteristics, which are of low value in the eyes of the native population, with an ascribed status of origin of equally low value, since they come from less developed contexts. The *Unterschichtung* tendency of immigration can be illustrated by means of census and survey data. From 1950 to 1960 the share of immigrants in the lower stratum has more than doubled. If the proportion of foreign unskilled workers of the total for this category is considered by itself we find that it has increased from 9.9 percent in 1950 to 39.0 percent in 1960. If the *saisonniers* are included this share amounts to even about 60 percent. In 1970 already 37.8 percent of all workers were foreigners, and with the inclusion of seasonal workers this figure rises to 45.8 percent. Although, due to a change in census cagetories, there are not exact figures on the number of unskilled foreign workers for 1970, one may safely assert that their share has increased further since 1960.

The figures indicate that the lower-lower stratum in Switzerland consists mainly of immigrants. On the other hand, this massive *Unterschichtung* opens up greater chances of upward social mobility for the native population. Table 6 illustrates the extent to which these chances have been used. While during 1950–1960 the native labor force increased

Table 5.   Unskilled, Semiskilled, and Skilled Workers in the Lower Stratum,
             Their Distribution, 1950-1970.

Year	Total, Swiss, and Foreigners		Swiss		Foreigners	
1950	1,068,814	(100.0%)	983,834	(87.9%)	128,980	(12.1%)
1960	1,271,973	(100.0%)	918,513	(72.2%)	353,460	(27.8%)
1970	1,352,690	(100.0%)	841,629	(62.2%)	511,061	(37.8%)

Source: Federal Censuses.

Table 6.   Increases in the Labor Force, 1950-1960 and 1960-1970.

	Total, Swiss and Foreigners	Swiss	Foreigners
1950-1960			
Workers	203,159	−21,321	224,480
	(56.9%)	(−19.3%)	(91.2%)
Middle and higher occupations	153,596	131,884	21,712
	(43.1%)	(119.3%)	(8.8%)
TOTAL	356,755	110,563	246,192
	(100.0%)	(100.0%)	(100.0%)
1960-1970			
Workers	80,717	−76,884	157,601
	(16.2%)	(−28.8%)	(68.3%)
Middle and higher occupations	417,405	344,265	73,140
	(83.8%)	(128.8%)	(31.7%)
TOTAL	498,122	267,381	230,741
	(100.0%)	(100.0%)	(100.0%)

Source: Federal Censuses

by 110,563, the increase in the middle and higher occupations was 131,884 and this trend is even more visible in the period 1960-1970. This points not only to a higher intergenerational—but also to a high intragenerational—upward mobility of the native population. This tendency is strongly supported by the findings of a survey carried out in the city of Zurich among Swiss belonging to the lower, the lower middle, and the middle–middle strata (Hoffmann-Nowotny, 1973:69–70). Considering these data it may be assumed that the individual upward mobility, which is very high even in comparison with other highly developed industrial societies (see Lipset and Bendix, 1966:25) has contributed toward reinforcing the societal emphasis put on the value of "mobility." All the more difficult then must be the situation of those nationals who, in spite of increased mobility chances and actually high mobility, have not or have only slightly participated in it. A second problem concerns the situation of nationals who have experienced a very rapid upward mobility, without however improving their occupational qualifications. The upward mobility of this latter group can be characterized as disequilibrated. Its members are exposed to a latent threat of downward mobility while the nonmobile nationals tend to interpret their situation in terms of a relative downward mobility since they find themselves on the same social level as the immigrants.

Both national groups react to this situation by developing a high degree of anomie (Hoffmann-Nowotny, 1973:ch. 3.1) setting in motion the well-known mechanisms of prejudice formation and discrimination against the immigrants. More interesting perhaps is another reaction: both groups tend to belittle the relevance of achievement criteria with regard to occupational positions and occupational mobility and to emphasize ascribed criteria such as membership of the native group. The more the values of

Table 7. Intergenerational Occupational Mobility Among Swiss: Comparison Between the Occupational Distributions of Fathers and Sons

Occupational Position	Fathers (%)	Sons (%)	Percent Difference
Worker	37.4	23.1	−14.3
Self-employed	35.9	11.0	−24.9
Employee/Civil servant	25.2	64.5	+39.3
Other	1.5	1.5	
TOTAL	100.0	100.0	(N = 473)

Table 8. Intragenerational Occupational Mobility Among Swiss: Comparison Between the First and Present Occupation.

Occupational Position	Fathers (%)	Sons (%)	Percent Difference
Worker	58.7	23.1	−35.6
Self-employed	2.7	11.0	+8.3
Employee/Civil servant	38.1	64.5	+26.4
Other	0.6	1.5	
TOTAL	100.0	100.0	(N = 473)

Table 9.   Intended Regulation of Dismissal from Jobs
Dependent on Emphasis on National Membership.

Who should be dismissed first?	Emphasis on National Membership			
	Low %	Medium %	High %	(N)
Foreigners	16.0	26.9	48.7	(148)
Bad workers	84.0	73.1	51.3	(318)
Total	100.0	100.0	100.0	
(N)	(169)	(108)	(189)	(466)

$x^2 = 45.58$ df = 2   gamma = $-.53$ $p < 0.001$

their own group are emphasized, the stronger is the tendency to replace achievement by ascribed criteria (Hoffmann-Nowotny, 1973:104).

Unterschichtung of a society and its consequences thus combine in creating a tendency which may be described as an attempt at "neo-feudalization" of a modern society: Social status distribution is not based on performance or capability but on membership in a certain ethnic group. It may be said therefore that immigration leads to reproducing the stratification of the international system in the immigration country and that one of its consequences consists in large parts of the native population desiring that this kind of stratification become stabilized. As has been said, this applies to the group who has experienced rapid and disequilibrated mobility as well as to the nonmobile group of nationals who see themselves in an underprivileged situation.

However, the attitudes of both groups do not coincide with regard to the question of the desirable number of foreigners. While 34.3 percent of the group mentioned first is in favor of a reduction in this number, the proportion of the second group advocating such a measure is 61.0 percent. A more refined analysis shows that the tendency to reject a reduction in the number of foreigners increases among those upward mobile nationals who have been pushed to a relatively high occupational level which immigrants cannot yet hope to achieve. So it appears that only the overprivileged group is convinced of the effectiveness of the neo-feudal model, i.e., they see in it an adequate protection of their status. The underprivileged group, on the other hand, sees the means for preserving their positions and averting the threat to their status only in enforced remigration.

This situation offers various forms of adaptation to the immigrants.

Since immigration into Switzerland is not meant to win the country new citizens but to import a labor force, it is obvious that the immigrant himself tries to avoid formal as well as informal discrimination by going back to his country. The answers to the questions put to a random sample of Italians in Zurich show that even among those who have spent 11 or more years in Switzerland 64.6 percent would remigrate to Italy if they could find an equally well paid job there and an equivalent occupation.

Table 10 clearly shows that the intention to remigrate depends on the perception of social discrimination (Hoffmann-Nowotny, 1973:259). It may seem surprising that even if the degree of perceived social discrimination is low, almost 60 percent of this category would consider remigration. However, considering the above-mentioned hypothesis and taking into account what has been said about Switzerland's own view of itself as an immigration country, the number of immigrants who see their emigration as definitive appears, on the contrary, as large.

Within a structural perspective the readiness to remigrate seems to be relatively high (65.1 percent) if, with a middle or higher education only a relatively low income has been obtained, while this readiness is comparatively low (44.7 percent) if, with a low education, a relatively high income has been achieved. The readiness to remigrate is also relatively low if the immigrants have adapted to the neo-feudal model offered them by the nationals, i.e., if they are willing to recognize that the better occupational positions are due to natives as such and that immigrants must be satisfied with the lower positions.

The neo-feudal model is accepted mainly by immigrants with a minimum of education and occupying the lowest positions as to income and occupation. The share of immigrants with neo-feudal attitudes increases with increasing stay, if the immigrants have not experienced

Table 10.   Intention to Remigrate Dependent
on Perceived Social Discrimination

Intention to Remigrate	Perceived Social Discrimination			
	Low %	Medium %	High %	(N)
Yes	59.3	79.6	90.6	(316)
No	40.7	20.4	9.4	(107)
Total	100.0	100.0	100.0	
N	(177)	(108)	(138)	(423)

$x^2 = 41.95$ df = 2   gamma = −.58   p < 0.001

Table 11.   Intention to Remigrate
Dependent on a Neo-feudal Attitude.

Intention to Remigrate	Neo-feudal Attitude		
	Yes %	No %	(N)
Yes	61.7	84.3	(325)
No	38.3	15.7	(102)
Total	100.0	100.0	
(N)	(154)	(273)	(427)

$x^2 = 26.34$ df $= 1$ gamma $= -.54$ $p < 0.001$

upward mobility and have therefore given up any further expectations of mobility. As with other forms of adaptation, this one too aims at reducing anomic tensions. Since the group of migrants under discussion can hardly hope to remigrate tensions are reduced by abandoning expectations of mobility.

Furthermore (Hoffmann-Nowotny, 1973:238–239), this group of immigrants emphasizes consumption goals instead of mobility chances, a fact which may be interpreted as an attempt at compensating a low social status and nonexistent mobility chances.

On the other hand, that form of adaptation which could be characterized as collective anomie is only just beginning to appear. Collective anomie here means the attempt at confronting tensions not on an individual but a collective basis and at taking measures in favor of collective mobility of the immigrants. At present such attempts are restricted to a small minority of immigrants. They are hampered by institutional barriers: the immigrants being noncitizens do not have a direct access to political processes. Moreover, organizational activities of foreigners are strictly limited. If the foreigner's permit of stay is for one year only it may simply not be renewed if he engages in activities considered unfavorably by the authorities. Apart from this, the analysis shows that due to their low educational level most immigrants do not have the conditions necessary for collective anomie. However, as rotation of immigrants is decreasing and duration of stay is therefore increasing, the chances for collectivizing anomie may increase too, if the chances of individual mobility should continue to remain limited.

This will depend not only on whether it is possible to reduce the discrimination practiced individually by the nationals against the immigrants but also on the legal status of the immigrants; a change in this latter status might provide them with the opportunity to break out of their marginality.

The legal status of immigrants is of great importance because the tendency of the nationals to discriminate against the immigrants is, of course, reinforced by the existence of laws containing special and discriminatory rules concerning immigrants.

THE LEGAL STATUS OF IMMIGRANTS

We have emphasized above that immigration into Switzerland is basically conceived of as an import of workers. This conception is first expressed by the absence of what could be called an immigration policy. Second, it is clearly expressed in the laws and rules concerning immigrants as well as in the administrative handling of these laws. When studying these laws it becomes clear that for dealing with problems belonging to the realm of immigration policy, only the instruments of a classical foreigners policy are available.[8] A foreigner who wants to immigrate into Switzerland first needs a work permit and then he gets a permit to stay. Provided the foreigner does not come as a *saisonnier,* his permit of stay is valid for one year. After that time he may have it prolonged for another year if he applies for it. After a stay of more than 5 years he gets a permit valid for 2 years. However, he has no legal claim to the prolongation of his permit; this is exclusively up at the discretion of the authorities. They may agree to extend it if the economy is flourishing and the labor market saturated and if the foreigner's behavior has not given rise to complaints. The permit to stay is valid only for the canton that has granted it[9] and for a certain job at a certain work place.

The crux of the Swiss restrictive policy are the regulations restricting movement of aliens in the country. In 1968, when the restrictive legislation reached its peak, the status quo of the annual permit holders was frozen for 5 years. That meant that a foreigner coming to Switzerland to work could not change his job, nor his occupation nor his residence (canton) for the next 5 years without losing his permit, which was tied to the status at the time of entry. Regulations issued in the subsequent years 1970, 1971 and 1973, reduced the minimum stay for the job to one year and occupation and canton stay to three. Certain employments were exempt, like those in the field of health care and in the tourist industry. The 1975 Regulations reduced all limits uniformly to one year to all yearly permit holders. These limits are federal and local or cantonal government may raise them. The permit holders have no right to have their permits extended.

All in all, the latest regulations represent a certain liberalization and an improvement of the status of foreign workers in Switzerland. Additional improvement can be seen in the fact that spouses of Swiss nationals are exempt from alien permit regulations and are set equal to the domiciled alien population.

In matters of naturalization, on the other hand, the situation did not improve at all. The Federal Act of September 29, 1952 (Art. 15, § 1), increased the number of years required for citizenship from six to 12; a ruling was added requiring a proof of assimilation.

The *saisonnier* as a rule may not change his work place or job either nor move to another canton. After a stay of 10 years the foreigner may ask to be granted a resident permit. If he is successful—after much scrutiny by the authorities—he will be the equal of the nationals as far as economic activities are concerned. Without interference from the authorities he may then freely choose his work place, his occupation and his place of residence; he may also pursue an independent profession.

The fact that the foreigner is not granted a permit to immigrate but only a limited permit to stay, and the fact that this permit depends on his first getting a permit to work, illustrates what we mentioned at the beginning of this section. In particular, that he must ask each year for an extension of his permit teaches the foreigner that his stay is only of a temporary character in the eyes of the immigration country. The curbs put on his changing work place, job and canton severely limited his mobility chances, until recently.

Table 12 shows that the immigrant's income strongly depends on the duration of his stay; the strong decrease in the low income category and the increase in the high income category after a stay of more than 5 years is particularly striking (at the time of the interviews changing work place and job was possible only after a stay of 5 years).

If in the relationship between duration of stay and income, education is controlled for, we find that the mobility chances opened up by the permission to change job, work place, and canton (after 5 years) are used more, the higher the educational level of the immigrant. This means, on the other hand, that by limiting these rights some of the foreigners were obliged for quite a while to work at jobs below their level of qualification. As an example of the effects these special rulings have on the attitudes of foreigners we will consider their political orientation.

As can be seen, the share of immigrants voting in favor of an extreme

Table 12.   Income Dependent on Duration of Stay.

Income	Less than 1 year %	1–2 years %	3–5 years %	6–10 years %	11 and more years %	(N)
Low	67.5	50.0	49.6	24.2	23.5	(171)
Medium	22.5	37.5	30.4	45.4	41.2	(178)
High	10.0	12.5	20.0	30.4	35.3	(116)
Total	100.0	100.0	100.0	100.0	100.0	
(N)	(40)	(48)	(115)	(194)	(68)	(465)

$x^2 = 49.02$ df = 8   gamma = .36 $p < 0.001$
Source: Hoffmann-Nowotny, 1973: 184.

socialist party increases until a stay of 5 years; after that it decreases rapidly.

Limiting the freedom of the foreigner during the first year of his stay (and during 5 years until recently) making his permission to stay dependent on his work permit, and committing him to a certain job at a certain work place—by all this the state places the employer in a strong position vis-à-vis his foreign employee. If, for instance, the foreigner is fired, he will lose his work permit and with it his permission to stay—he must leave the country. This dependency is often exploited, even after the barred period has expired. To illustrate this: if the employee gives up his job and if the employer then informs unfavorably on his behavior, this

Table 13.   Income[a] (Category "High") Dependent on Education and Duration of Stay.

	Education			
Duration of Stay	Low %	Medium %	High %	% Diff.
Until 5 years	11.0 (91)	17.4 (69)	28.2 (39)	−17.2
More than 5 years	24.0 (129)	34.0 (97)	57.6 (33)	−33.6
% Diff.	−13.0	−16.6	−29.4	
x^2	5.16	4.83	5.19	
df	1	1	1	
gamma	.44	.42	.55	
p	<0.05	<0.05	<0.05	

Source: Hoffmann-Nowotny, 1973:185.
[a] For the multivariate analysis the variable "income" was dichotomized, income-low: until 1200 Sfrs.: income-high: more than 1,200.00 Sfrs.

Table 14.   Party Affinity (PCI/PSIUP) Dependent on Duration of Stay.

	Duration of Stay				
	Less than 1 year %	1–2 years %	3–5 years %	6–10 years %	11 and more years %
Party affinity Voting for PCI/PSIUP[a]	20.0	27.1	29.1	20.8	14.9

may cause the authorities to revoke his permission to stay or, more simply, not to extend it. Other curbs on the rights of foreigners concern the family. At present—an improvement on the past—a foreigner who is obliged to apply each year for a new permit may have his family join him after he has spent 12 months in Switzerland. Exceptions are made only for foreigners in high positions. *Saisonniers* may not have their families living with them at all.

In order to get permission to have his family join him, the foreigner must prove that he has adequate living quarters and is in a position to maintain his children. The living quarters may not be obtained at the expense of a national having to move out. In such a case the foreigner would not be permitted to have his family live with him.

In the year 1970, the number of foreigners accepted in Switzerland was limited officially. Since then the discriminatory rules are gradually being mitigated. In the long run, foreigners are supposed to have full freedom, becoming the equals of nationals on the labor market and in freedom of choice of their residence canton. At what future point in time the last barriers will be removed is, however, hard to say.

Concerning the work laws and social laws, no difference is made between foreigners and nationals. The foreigner has a claim to old-age pension and he is insured against disability, though even here there are some special rulings. As to unemployment, until recently, only those foreigners were insured, as a rule, who have a resicence permit, i.e., who have lived in Switzerland for more than 10 years. This regulation, however, was also changed, and today the holders of a yearly permit are also insured against unemployment.

Since the exertion of political rights is associated with citizenship and since citizenship is obtained only after many years and after many barriers have been crossed the immigrant has practically no political rights. Since political activity by foreigners is looked upon as interfering with Swiss interior policy, the foreigner is prevented from articulating his interests in an organized way. Due to the lack of citizenship the usual channels of interest articulation via political parties and voting are closed to the immigrants and the activities of their organizations are narrowly limited. Up to now these organizations have not played any important part in the process of political articulation, and are quite powerless.

The attempt to give these organizations at least a consultative status has not been seriously considered at the political level and probably has no chance of being realized even in the long run. Thus the immigrant remains a mere object of decisions taken by the authorities. Incidentally, the foreigner, apart from a few exceptions, may not even vote in the church communities, though he pays the same church taxes as the nationals.

Foreigners without a residence permit are also treated differently in terms of the way their income tax is calculated and paid. While nationals submit a tax declaration every two years, income tax of the foreigner is directly deducted from his weekly or monthly salary by his employer. This means that instead of individual deductions being made from taxes (for household, children, etc.) there are deductions according to type. Because of this, the foreigners concerned pay, as a rule, more taxes than a comparable group of nationals. Foreigners with a comparatively high income are excepted from direct deduction of taxes; the income limit is fixed variously by the different cantons (in the canton of Zurich it is 36,000 Sfrs. per year). Also, foreign children have to struggle with a number of problems. One of the main ones results from the ambiguous attitude of Swiss authorities as to whether they consider immigration as definitive or not. The same attitude prevails in the emigration countries which in turn emphasize that they consider emigration as basically temporary. This double insecurity is reflected in the attitude of the immigrants which Braun (1970:437ff) characterizes by means of the concept of *Heimkehrillusion* (illusion to return).

The educational system and the teachers struggle with the question of whether the children of foreigners should be prepared for definitive residence in the immigration country or whether they should be socialized with a view to remigration or whether both possibilities should be left open. In spite of the generally held view that immigration is to be considered as temporary the Swiss educational system has chosen the first alternative. Thus the children of immigrants are obliged to go to the public schools where, as a rule, they are taught side by side with the nationals. Several cantons have made an exception and granted permission to establish private schools, but the number is low. In addition to the usual classes in the public schools, part of the foreign children are taught their mother tongue in special classes, an activity organized and paid for mainly by the foreign consulates. According to the teachers, these additional classes represent a heavy burden for the children, hampering their performance in the public school. Thus, while in general there is no formal discrimination against foreign children, it is easy to understand why they are usually below the standard of native children and rarely succeed in going on to middle or higher education.

The low educational level of the parents, their deficient knowledge of the language of the immigration country and the children's own language difficulties are only some of the factors interfering with school integration and equality of opportunity. While in several places there are programs aimed at reducing the disadvantaged position of foreign children, these programs reach only a minority of children due mainly to a lack of teachers, financial resources, or political goodwill. So the assumption that the foreign children will simply grow up to form a new sub-proletariat, replicating that of their parents, probably will be confirmed.

THE POLITICAL CONSEQUENCES OF IMMIGRATION

It has been said earlier in this discussion that one of the consequences of immigration into Switzerland consists in an increase in the level of anomie among the nationals. On the individual level anomie is expressed in discrimination against the immigrants, a tendency which is reinforced by official legal discrimination. These anomic tendencies have recently acquired an organized political articulation. In order to understand these processes it is necessary briefly to illustrate the plebiscitary character of Swiss democracy. Two plebiscitary instruments are of particular importance: (1) the *Gesetzesreferendum,* and (2) the *Verfassungsinitiative.* By means of the *Gesetzesreferendum* the government can be forced to submit a law which has been passed in parliament to popular vote. If the law is rejected by the simple majority of the voters and the cantons it must be withdrawn. On the federal level, any law must be submitted to popular vote if this is demanded by 50,000 (until recently, 30,000) citizens. On the other hand, there is no possibility of forcing the government or parliament to pass a certain rule or law. In other words, the "Referendum" is always only a second step.

On the federal level and with the support of 100,000 (until recently, 50,000) citizens, the government can be forced to submit to popular vote a demand for changing or supplementing the constitution. Due to this possibility subjects pertaining to the realm of law can be incorporated into the constitution, and thus become binding on parliament and government. Immigration is such a case. As early as the mid-1960s certain Swiss groups asked for a reduction, a limitation or even a reversal. In 1965 the ''Demokratische Partei'' of the canton of Zurich formally requested that the constitution contain an article ruling that the maximum number of foreigners should not exceed 10 percent of the resident population. In order to come down to this limit the number of foreigners would have to have been reduced by 5 percent annually. After the government, under pressure from this initiative, had agreed to reduce the share of foreigners, the initiative was withdrawn in 1968: no popular vote took place.

Later it became evident that the measures taken by the government were insufficient: the number of foreigners continued to increase. In 1968 the Nationale Aktion gegen die Ueberfremdung von Volk und Heimat (the literal translation is: National Action against the Over-Foreignization of the People and the Fatherland) demanded that the share of foreigners be reduced to 10 percent of the native resident population, a goal they proposed to reach within 4 years. Furthermore, they requested that no Swiss citizen be fired by any firm that employed foreigners in the same occupational category. In 1970, this initiative was voted upon and was defeated by the small margin of 54 percent (no) to 46 percent (yes).

This time, again under pressure, the government implemented efficient measures in order to stabilize the number of foreigners. However, before these measures really became effective, the economic recession set in during 1974 and rather drastically reduced the number of foreigners, as shown in Table 1. In spite of the stabilization policy which had kept the number of foreigners to approximately one million, the National Aktion started a new initiative in 1972, asking for a reduction by 50 percent in the number of foreigners. If accepted, 500,000 foreigners would have had to leave Switzerland. This initiative, however, was defeated 2:1 in 1974.

After their relative success in 1970 the originators of this initiative formed two political parties, the Nationale Aktion and the Republikanische Bewegung, both on the extreme right. In 1971 both parties participated in the election of the Nationalrat (Chamber of Deputies). They succeeded in winning 10 out of 200 seats. Meantime, both parties have participated in a number of cantonal and communal elections and have been rather successful.

In 1972, the Republikanische Bewegung in turn started another attack against Ueberfremdung (over-foreignization) similar to the initiative voted upon in 1970. It was defeated 7:3 in 1977, together with two other initiatives which had been launched by the Nationale Aktion. These votes prove that a majority of the Swiss is not willing to support the extreme policy of the "over-foreignizaiton" parties, but that nevertheless a however declining considerable proportion of the native population can be mobilized by these parties.

In the fall of 1973, the movement of Catholic workers and employees began to collect signatures for a new initiative running contrary to the rightist ones. This represents a first approach to something resembling an immigration policy. It assumes that the number of foreigners will remain unchanged for the moment and goes on to emphasize the measures to be taken in order to integrate the immigrants. However, it took 4 years before the necessary 50,000 signatures were collected. It has not yet been decided when the vote on this initiative will take place.

While I emphasized at the beginning the fact that the problem of immigrant minorities is similar in all Western European countries, I have pointed to a particularly Swiss character to the problem: its politicization. This phenomenon which, as noted, has even led to the emergence of two new political parties must be interpreted as a consequence of the plebiscitary character of Swiss democracy. This particular circumstance allows for direct mobilization of the anomic potential. This means for parliament and government that the transition from a policy for foreigners to an immigration policy—whose necessity is gradually being understood—is almost made impossible or at minimum requires utmost caution. Any measure which could be interpreted as serving to improve the situation of the immigrants will be strongly opposed and will only provoke the further mobilization of a part of the native population.

There is hardly any need to emphasize the fact that the initiatives taken against over-foreignization, following one upon another, and their drastic demands affect the attitudes of immigrants. Their insecurity, already great enough for legal reasons, is increased by public discussion about the initiatives against over-foreignization. That under these circumstances the immigrants' efforts at integration and assimilation are reduced almost to nil is hardly surprising.

THE FUTURE OF THE FOREIGN WORKER PROBLEM

One can summarize this question, which is identical with questions about the future of foreign national minorities in Switzerland, by saying that their future is almost exclusively determined by whether it is possible to solve the problems which immigration is creating for nationals. Only then would it be feasible to abolish the remaining discriminatory rulings and to transform gradually the policy toward foreigners into an immigration policy. Whether such a policy would succeed in reducing the waiting period prescribed for naturalization and in mitigating other rulings concerning naturalization is doubtful, however. All that may be expected realistically is a reduction in the waiting time until the residence permit is granted. The residence permit gives the foreigner the right to reside permanently in Switzerland; legally, he becomes the equal of the nationals, but he has no political rights. It may be supposed that most foreigners would see in this solution an acceptable compromise for the near future.

However, the problems of organized interest articulation of foreigners and of the place such an organization could find in political decision making would remain unsolved. Because of this, it hardly matters whether these interests result from the immigrant's situation as an immigrant or from his/her being a member of the lower stratum. A Swiss political party explicity advocating the interest of the immigrants would suffer today a loss of voters. This could be avoided only if it were possible to reduce the tensions among nationals to such a degree that they could afford to be indifferent to the activities of such a party. However, whether a political party would be willing to advocate immigrant interests with no hope of winning votes, since the persons having these interests cannot vote, is another question. This again points to the difference between Switzerland and the classical immigration countries, such as the United States of America, where immigrants represent a considerable voting potential that can be mobilized by political parties.

A cynic might be tempted to say that the problems of those members of the minority most affected by discrimination could be "solved"—by abolishing their status as a minority, sending them home. Since the initiatives failed, the aliens were not forced by political means to remigrate. But perhaps it was not much of a difference to those who had to return to their home countries because they lost their jobs as a consequence of the economic recession.

NOTES

1. There are four national languages officially recognized in the federal constitution: German (mother tongue of 74.5 percent of the Swiss citizens), French (20.1 percent), Italian (4.0 percent) and Romansh (1.0 percent).

2. It is probably not commonly known that despite the fact that Switzerland is highly developed, the existing internal development differences are considerable. The total Swiss GNP per capita is 13,165 SFr., but the GNP p.c. in the canton of Basel-Stadt is 19,815

SFr. and in the canton of Appenzell Inner Rhodes 8,825 SFr. (according to estimates made by the Union Bank of Switzerland, 1971).

3. This means that foreigners enter Swiss society at the very bottom and form a new lower stratum.

4. A distinction is made between (1) foreigners with a residence permit, (2) foreigners with a permit to stay, and (3) foreigners allowed to work on a seasonal basis (*saisonniers*). As a rule, a residence permit is granted after a continuous stay of 10 years. There is no time limit to the residence permit; it can be revoked only in exceptional cases. The permit to stay is limited. When granted for the first time, the limit is one year. The permit to work on a seasonal basis is granted as a rule for 9 months.

5. Swiss citizenship is achieved through becoming a citizen of a canton and a community. The communal assembly or the communal parliament vote on granting or rejecting the application of the candidate. In a procedure taking about two years the candidate is scrutinized. Any foreigner who has lived in Switzerland for at least 12 years may apply for citizenship. The duration of this period may be extended by individual cantons; moreover, the communities have special residence requirements. The charges for naturalization are quite considerable. In the canton of Geneva, for instance, they vary between 300 and 75,000 Swiss francs; in the canton of Vaud the maximum charge is 10 percent of annual income.

6. In 1970, already 37 percent of the foreign resident population had a permit of residence, i.e., they have been in Switzerland for more than 10 years. In April 1978 this figure amounted to 72 percent.

7. For the following, see also Hoffmann-Nowotny (1970 and 1973) and Heintz and Hoffmann-Nowotny (1969).

8. Incidentally, this is not a particularity of Switzerland. The same exists in other Western European immigration countries, such as Germany, which in the last few years has received nearly four million immigrants. Germany, too, pursues an antinaturalization policy, trying to limit the stay of foreigners to a certain number of years.

9. This does not imply, of course, that the foreigner may not travel, only that he must have his residence in the canton granting the permit.

REFERENCES

Almond, Gabriel L. and G. Bingham Powell
1966   Comparative Politics; A Developmental Approach. Boston: Little Brown.
Bericht des Bundesrates an die Bundesversammlung über das zweite Volksbegehren
1969   gegen die Ueberfremdung. Bern.
Bickel, Wilhelm
1947   Bevölkerungsgeschichte und Bevölkerungspolitik in der Schweiz seit dem Ausgang des Mittelalters. Zurich.
Braun, Rudolf
1970   Sozio-kulturelle Probleme der Eingliederung italienischer Arbeitskräfte in der Schweiz. Erlenbach-Zurich Eugen Rentsch.
Heintz, Peter and Hans-Joachim Hoffmann-Nowotny
1960   "Das Fremdarbeiterproblem aus soziologischer Sicht." Schweizer Monatshefte, 49 (5):466–473.

Hoffmann-Nowotny, Hans-Joachim
1970   Migration, Ein Beitrag zu einer soziologischen Erklärung, Stuttgart, Ferd.
        Enke.
Hoffmann-Nowotny, Hans-Joachim
1973   Soziologie des Fremdarbeiterproblems, Eine theoretische und empirische
        Analyse am Beispiel der Schweiz (with a summary in English, French and
        Italian). Stuttgart, Ferd. Enke.
Lehmbruch, Gerhard
1967a   Proporzdemokratie, Politisches System und Politische Kultur in der Schweiz
        und in Oesterreich. Tubingen.
Lehmbruch, Gerhard
1967b   "A non-competitive pattern of conflict management in liberal democracies: the
        case of Switzerland, Austria and Lebanon." Presented at the Seventh World
        Congress of the International Political Science Association, Brussels.
Lijphart, Arend
1967   "Typologies of democratic systems." Presented at the Seventh World Congress
        of the International Political Science Association, Brussels.
Lipset, Seymour M. and Reinhard Bendix
1966   Social Mobility in Industrial Society. Berkeley: University of Cal.
Rokkan, Stein
1970   "Foreword." In Jurg Steiner, Gewaltlose Politik und kulturelle Vielfalt,
        Hypothesen entwickelt am Beispiel der Schweiz. Bern and Stuttgart: Paul
        Haupt.

ASCRIPTION AND INTERGROUP RELATIONS:
THE IMPACT OF LEGAL AND
POLITICAL CHANGES

VIJAI P. SINGH

Ascription is pivotal in understanding changes in racial and caste inequality in the United States and India. It is generally assumed that
relevance of ascribed principles governing social relations declines as
societies evolve into more differentiated social systems (Parsons, 1964:
342–345). What is not sufficiently clear are the mechanisms that different
societies choose to overcome ascriptive inequalities without seriously
disrupting their functioning. Ascriptive principles have been used as a
rationalization in dealing with many complex problems even though they
seemed unjustifiable and morally wrong. It is mainly because ascription
has considerable staying power and provides cheap solutions with reason-

Research in Race and Ethnic Relations, Volume 2, pages 97–114
Copyright © 1980 by JAI Press Inc.
All rights of reproduction in any form reserved.
ISBN: 0-89232-141-5

able reliability (Mayhew, 1970: 313-314). Those in superior positions obtain benefits through the actual use or the threat of coercion as well as voluntary accord.

Kemper's (1974: 844-853) distinction of reference points of ascription are important in this context. The first type rests on the performance capacity of the actor, such as age and sex, which are part of the division of labor. The second type, which includes race, religion, ethnicity, place of birth and citizenship, is neither based on performance nor part of the division of labor. Kemper attempts to answer the question, "How is it that positions in the division of labor are assigned on grounds other than performance capacity?" by suggesting differential distribution of power. Apparently, those with greater power influence the context and modes of socialization of the less powerful and create conditions of willing compliance by the latter. The key to understanding the nonperformance aspects of ascription through the distribution of power reflects a preoccupation with status consistency which in this instance means any change in relative position of racial or caste groups must be consistent with the distribution of power. Obviously power is important in maintaining ascriptive inequality, and its redistribution may alter certain aspects of social and economic relations. But it would be too simplistic to assume that ascriptive inequality is dependent on power.

Even in contemporary India the political and economic power of non-Brahmins has not resulted in a massive readjustment of caste hierarchies. The mobility within the caste system through the process of Sanskritization (Srinivas, 1966: 552-560) involving emulation of life styles of upper castes by the lower castes has remained largely a theoretical possibility. The greater power of non-Brahmins may have made Brahmins tactfully polite in some situations but has not created a new deference structure altering traditional ritual relations. Even though the caste system has been legally abolished and higher castes officially do not enjoy any legal privileges, claims of superior ritual status by economically and politically powerful lower castes are vigorously resisted. It is even more difficult for the untouchables. Blacks in the United States holding political offices are not immune to social discrimination by whites in private domains.

Some aspects of relations have value primacy over others. This duality of "encompassing" and "encompassed" provides a useful framework within which the relationship between ascribed status and power can be interpreted (Dumont, 1967: 32-33; 1970). Caste hierarchy in India and racial hierarchy in the United States within the cultural system can be assumed to be all-encompassing and need not be dependent on power. Thus, esteem, reputation and other advantages which are not based on performance are also not necessarily based on the distribution of power. Comparing untouchables in India and blacks in the United States on economic and political dimensions, one would find that their formal political participation is more acceptable to the dominant groups in the society than is equality in social and economic relations. The staying power of ascription, its being cheap and functional, lies not in the distribution of power but in the value system of the society. The voluntary acceptance of one's subordinate status can best be explained by examining the customs and traditions which are displayed through symbols in relevant interaction situations.

The formal participation of the disadvantaged groups in political institutions need not produce greater equality in social relations. It may even lead to greater autonomy between social status and political power in the sense that racial, ethnic and caste distinctions become more significant in marriage, choice of friends and place of residence. The ascriptive identity in this context is used to maintain and promote group solidarity and cooperation to maximize advantages in economic and power relations. What we must understand is that the principle of political equality need not be accompanied by social or economic equality. Social, economic and political inequalities interact and influence each other, but for the blacks in the United States and the untouchables in India complete social equality is still too distant. Apparently the dominant groups in both societies do not seem to be willing to favor public policy involving sacrifices on their part for a prolonged period of time to promote the social and economic welfare of the disadvantaged groups. As the hopes and expectations of blacks in the United States and untouchables in India have risen, so have open resistance and outcry by many members of the dominant groups in the form of court battles, public demonstrations and occasionally even violence.

It is under this general framework that we will examine the nature of ascriptive inequality in India and the United States, the Civil Rights Acts, compensatory privileges, responses of dominants groups and the dilemma for the public policy to bring about equality of results through the equality of opportunity.

ASCRIPTIVE INEQUALITY IN INDIA AND THE UNITED STATES

In an ideal caste society one's position is determined on the basis of birth in one of the ranked groups and mobility is impossible. Parentage determines group membership, and a particular life style develops as a consequence of residential separation, greater interaction with members of one's own group and less contact with others, segregated occupational participation and socialization preparing individuals to behave appropriate to their respective ranks. In essence, the individual shares the collective destiny of his/her group and must accept the rationale or ideology supporting the existing structure of opportunity. This helps in maintaining the status quo and also assures that privileged groups will continue to maintain their entitlement for the good things of life.

This ideal conception of the caste system has not existed in reality anywhere. The closest to this conception was the traditional caste system in India which has been undergoing radical changes since independence. Even in India, there was no convincing evidence that all lower-caste persons accepted their inferior position or that the upper castes maintained their privileges without a challenge. Intimidation and coercion were often used to maintain the status quo. These became apparent as soon as social and political mobilization began at the turn of this century. Enormous amounts of human resources were lost by limiting opportunities and aspirations of the disadvantaged groups. The social division has continued even though the rationale supporting the caste system was on its way out.

The main sources of stigma for the untouchables were their so-called defiling characteristics in which they transmitted undesirable qualities to higher-caste persons upon contact. This partly resulted in their exclusion from desirable occupations, temples, drinking-water wells, and meeting halls. Residential patterns reflected existing social and economic organization. The untouchables lived in separate hamlets insulated from social interaction with higher castes. Segregation was widely practiced except in economic areas where cheap untouchable labor was needed to carry out agricultural activities and provide other services which no other caste wanted to perform (Mandelbaum, 1970: 339–340). They were the most economically depressed group in India. Village councils maintained order by enforcing traditional caste norms when untouchables refused to perform the most demeaning and least rewarding occupations. The government machinery deliberately ignored the plight of untouchables. Upper castes used intimidation and violence whenever untouchables took some initiative in improving their social and economic well-being. They were systematically discouraged from going to school, and the school environment was hostile toward their children. Their social and economic dependency and stereotyping had a negative impact on the aspirations of the children and many of them simply could not withstand the open harassment.

Despite the general consensus about the low status of untouchables, there was overwhelming evidence that they conformed to caste norms under tremendous political and economic pressures. They developed their own religious tradition based on equality and liberty. Many of them joined Christianity and Sikhism in an attempt to overcome the stigma they suffered under Hinduism and hoped that they would become part of a larger community. But soon they discovered that they were treated as untouchables by many members of their new faith. Those who did not convert went to law courts to obtain the rights to enter Hindu temples for worship and to use public facilities.

The caste system has not been restricted only to the Indian subcontinent But the Indian caste system is far more complex than the dual caste system of the United States (Dollard, 1937: 61–96); Berreman, 1960: 120–127; Singh 1976: 292–301). The dual caste system can be conceptualized when we look at the Indian society consisting of untouchables and non-untouchables. The cultural idioms that define caste in different situations are most difficult to alter. They were developed and institutionalized over many generations and have been supported by well-established customs and traditions. It is for these reasons that changes in economic and political conditions may not produce a dramatic reduction in social inequality between blacks and whites in the United States and untouchables and upper castes in India in the foreseeable future.

The top and bottom of the hierarchy was fixed, and lines between blacks and whites in the United States and untouchables and upper castes in India were maintained through economic and political dependency and social segregation. Even though blacks have enjoyed a greater degree of social equality than untouchables in India, their lower position in society was determined more by customs and traditions than by law—important attributes of the caste system. Also, they were unable to escape negative social evaluation due to their racial characteristics and other cumulative disadvantages. They suffered from systematic discrimination in education, occupation, housing, political participation, use of public transportation, use of public facilities and administration of justice until recently, mainly as a consequence of their ascribed characteristics. The caste system in the United States may not be as rigid, but "just as in India, it is preferable to be a Brahmin rather than Harijan (untouchable) regardless of economic class, in the United States it is preferable to be white rather than black..." (Duberman, 1976: 235). Both were subjected to negative stereotypes, myths and symbols. In other words, there were similarities between the caste systems of the two societies. The important difference lay in the use of religious and moral principles in

India and color in the United States for the justification and perpetuation of ascriptive inequality.

COMPENSATORY POLICY IN INDIA

The leaders of the Indian National Congress during the movement for Indian independence realized that untouchable leaders and spokesmen were unwilling to give their support without some promise of compensatory privileges for their community. Part of the negotiated resolution read as follows:

> Amongst Hindus, no one shall be regarded as an untouchable by reason of his birth, and those who have been so regarded hitherto will have the same right as other Hindus in regard to the use of public institutions. This right will have statutory recognition at the first opportunity and shall be one of the earliest acts of the Swaraj parliament, if it shall not have received such recognition before to secure, by every legitimate and peaceful means, an early removal of all social disabilities now imposed by custom upon the so-called untouchable classes, including the bar in respect of admission to temples (Tendulkar, 1961: 174).

Abolition of untouchability and special measures to improve the conditions of untouchables became the official policy of the Indian National Congress and were implemented through constitutional provisions as follows (Government of India, 1974: 97–98):

(i) the abolition of "untouchability" and the forbidding of its practice in any form (art. 17);

(ii) the promotion of their educational and economic interests and their protection from social injustice and all forms of exploitation (art. 46);

(iii) the throwing open by law of Hindu religious institutions of a public character to all classes and sections of Hindus (art. 25);

(iv) the removal of any disability, liability restriction or condition with regard to access to shops, public restaurants, hotels and places of public entertainment or the use of wells, tanks, bathing ghats, roads and places of public resort maintained wholly or partly out of State funds or dedicated to the use of the general public (art. 15);

(v) the curtailment by law, in the interests of any scheduled tribe, of the general rights of all citizens to move freely, settle in, and acquire property (art. 19 (5));

(vi) the forbidding of any denial of admission to educational institutions maintained by the State or receiving aid out of State funds (art. 29);

(vii) permitting the State to make reservation for the backward classes in public services in case of inadequate representation and requiring the State to consider the claims of the scheduled caste* and tribes in the making of appointments to public services (arts. 16 and 335);

(viii) special representation in Parliament and the State legislatures to scheduled
castes and tribes till 25 January 1980 (arts. 330, 332 and 334);

(ix) the setting up of advisory councils and separate departments in the States and
the appointment of a special officer at the Centre to promote their welfare and
safeguard their interests (Fifth Schedule and arts. 164 and 338);

(x) special provision for the administration and control of scheduled and tribal
areas (art. 244 and fifth and sixth schedules).

The office of the President of India has identified the scheduled castes
and scheduled tribes under articles 341 and 342. The states have been
advised to use economic criteria in determining other backward classes.
These constitutional provisions ensured equality before the law for all
persons and prohibited discrimination on the basis of birth or membership
in a particular group. The long-held practice of untouchability was out-
lawed and violators were to be punished under legal provisions.

THE QUOTA SYSTEM IN INDIA

The total population of India in 1971 was 547,949,809 and untouchables
constituted 79,995,896 persons distributed across India. Table 1 indicates
that one out of seven persons is an untouchable spread over 20 states and
7 union territories. The democratic system of government and growing
political awareness toward equality and justice among them sent clear
signals to the political leaders that special provisions would have to be
made for their immediate and effective participation in the political system.
In the context of negative stereotypes and their exclusion from political
participation for centuries, it was realized that the voting rights and freedom to run for political office would not guarantee adequate political
representation and a voice in the affairs of state. Therefore, articles
330 and 332 of the constitution provided that seats be reserved for untouchables (scheduled castes) in the national parliament and state legislatures in proportion to their population (see Table 1). This special provision was to continue only for the first 10 years from the date of its
commencement but was subsequently extended through amendments
until January 1980. In April 1980, it was extended again for another ten
years. This allows untouchables to take advantage of reservation of seats
continuously for forty years—more than a generation. At the village level,
state governments instituted statutory and administrative procedures for
their representation in the local bodies charged with the responsibility for
adjudicating local disputes and helping implement programs for social and
economic development.

Table 1.   Population distribution of Untouchables across States and Union
Territories with Reserved Seats in Parliament, State Legislatures, and Union
Territories Based on 1971 Census*

	Scheduled Castes	Parliament		State Legislatures	
		Total Number of Seats	Seats Reserved for Scheduled Castes	Total Number of Seats	Seats Reserved for Scheduled Castes
India	79,995,896				
States					
Andhra Pradesh	5,774,548	41	6	287	40
Assam	912,557	14	1	114	8
Bihar	7,950,652	53	7	318	45
Gujarat	1,825,432	24	2	168	11
Haryana	1,895,933	9	2	81	15
Himachal Pradesh	769,572	4	1	68	16
Jammu & Kashmir	381,277	6	—	75	6
Karnataka	3,850,034	27	4	216	29
Kerala	1,772,168	19	2	133	11
Madhya Pradesh	5,453,690	37	5	296	39
Maharashtra	3,025,761	45	3	270	15
Manipur	16,376	2	—	60	1
Meghalaya	3,887	2	—	60	—
Nagaland	—	1	—	52	—
Orissa	3,310,854	20	3	140	22
Punjab	3,348,217	13	3	104	23
Rajasthan	4,075,580	23	4	184	31
Tamil Nadu	7,315,595	39	7	234	42
Tripura	192,860	2	—	60	6
Uttar Pradesh	18,548,916	85	18	425	89
West Bengal	8,816,028	40	8	280	55
Union Territories					
Andaman & Nicobar Islands	—	1	—	—	—
Arunachal Pradesh	339	1	—	—	—
Chandigarh	29,073	1	—	—	—
Dadra & Nagar Haveli	1,332	1	—	—	—
Delhi	635,698	7	1	56	7
Goa, Daman & Diu	16,514	2	—	30	—
Lakshadweep	—	1	—	—	—
Mizoram	82	1	—	30	—
Pondicherry	72,921	1	—	30	5
TOTAL		522	77	3,771	516

*Government of India, 1974: 100 and 104 (derived from Tables 9.3 and 9.4).

Untouchables were engaged in jobs that required hard physical labor, that were demeaning and provided only bare minimum sustenance. The upper castes monopolized prestigious and lucrative occupations that excluded untouchables completely. In addition, untouchables remained largely illiterate and only a small fraction of those living in urban areas had acquired some education. Obviously it would take decades or possibly generations to remove various disabilities, and might take even longer before they fully enter the mainstream of the national life (Rosen, 1967: 195–207; Singh, 1976: 121–135). There were many occupations employing thousands of people at various levels of government which required little skill but had hardly any representation from the untouchables. Even if untouchables acquired some education and sought jobs appropriate to their skills, it was believed that they would be overwhelmed by overqualified higher-caste persons in the competition. Discriminatory attitudes of some of those charged with the responsibility for recruitment complicated further any hopes of ecnomic participation by the untouchables.

Therefore, reservation of seats in government services was instituted. States were free to reserve seats in case of inadequate representation without the requirement of consulting the Public Service Commission. According to the guidelines, 15 percent of the vacancies were reserved for untouchables in which competition on an all-India basis was required. In addition, 16.66 percent of the seats were reserved for other types of recruitment. For most categories of government jobs, 15 percent of the promotions were reserved for untouchables. Such requirements as age, standards of suitability and selection were to be relaxed to promote the representation of this group, provided that the persons selected were not unfit for the position.

Despite these efforts, a large number of positions reserved for untouchables remained unfilled mainly because of insufficient numbers of qualified candidates. The central government has been operating career planning and guidance and pre-employment coaching at the four major regional Centers throughout the country. A massive scholarship program has been in effect for many years. At present about 1,090,000 untouchable students are receiving post-high school scholarships every year. Pre-examination coaching centers have been established to prepare those appearing for various competitive examinations. The results of these efforts have been encouraging (Government of India, 1974: 103).

In one systematic study (Aggarwal and Ashraf, 1976: 175–192) it was reported that an overwhelming majority of untouchables in the sample wanted educational and occupational privileges to continue indefinitely.

People were aware of special scholarship programs and two-thirds of the recipients found it easy to obtain them. But there was underrepresentation in higher occupations and overrepresentation in low-level occupations. It was found that only 12 percent of households benefited from the job reservation policy even though 45 percent of them were actually eligible. Most of the respondents knew of reserved seats in parliament and state legislatures for their community. They were also aware of laws against untouchability but only 25 percent of them were familiar with the legal details. Nearly 95 percent of respondents felt that the grip of untouchability had not eased for them and the most severe discimination was found in the sharing of public facilities and entry to the Hindu temples.

But the numerical quota system for the untouchables and other minorities did not go unchallenged. The main source of resentment was the selection of possibly less qualified untouchables over more qualified high-caste Hindus. A simialr situation prevailed in reservation of seats in medical and engineering colleges. The uncertainty continued until 1951, when the Supreme Court of India ruled numerical quota systems unconstitutional. Subsequently this led to a constitutional amendment which stated that reservation of seats for educationally, economically and socially backward groups was proper but which prohibited a quota system purely on a communal basis. But the battle was far from over. The higher castes continued to challenge these provisions in higher courts throughout the land on various technical grounds. One typical observation of a court is reported as follows (Srinivas, 1969: 110):

> On July 31, 1962, the Mysore Government issued an order providing for reservation of 68% of seats in medical and engineering colleges for backward classes and Scheduled Castes and Tribes. The order listed 81 "backward classes" and 135 "more backward classes." In striking down the order two months later the Supreme Court declared that it was "a fraud on the Constitution." The judgment held that the classification of backward classes on the sole basis of caste was not permitted by article 15 (4). Furthermore, the reservation was clearly excessive, as it reduced the field of general competition to a mere 32% of the seats. The special provision, in other words, had so weakened the fundamental rule (equality of opportunity) as to rob it of most of its significance.

Unprecedented confrontation throughout the country between high caste Hindus and untouchables took place on the compensation policy of the government during 1977–1978. The press quoting government sources reported that more than 350 untouchables were killed throughout India in the year ending March 1978. In the state of Uttar Pradesh, where untouchables are most numerous, there were 174 deaths and 5,755 other crimes committed against them. Organized demonstrations and violence by high-caste Hindus against untouchables occurred in several states, most notably in Bihar and Uttar Pradesh to protest upward change in the numerical job quotas reserved for the latter by the state governments. On August 30, 1978, about 5,000 farmers from a nearby village came to New Delhi to protest the allotment of land by the government to landless untouchables. The latter had been tilling their land under police protection while a large group of high-caste farmers were sent to jail for their actions. Subsequently, some 15,000 farmers from the neighboring states of Punjab, Haryana, Rajasthan and Utter Pradesh staged demonstrations at the vilalge to show their support for the protesting farmers (Hindustan Times, September 7. 1978: 3). Such incidents seem to have become more common and crimes against untouchables so numerous in recent years that the commissioner for scheduled castes and tribes recommended the establishment of special courts at the state level for speedy trials. Quick resolution would bring punishment to those who violated Civil Rights Acts, especially involving untouchability. State governments did not show much enthusiasm for th is course of action. The central government in the meantime established a Minorities Commission in January 1978 to help implement various constitutional and other provisions to promote the welfare of the minority groups including the untouchables. The commission is charged with following functions:

1. To evaluate the working of the various safeguards provided in the Constitution for the protection of minorities and in laws passed by the Union and State governments.
2. To make recommendations with a view to ensuring effective implementation and enforcement of all the safeguards and the laws.
3. To undertake a review of the implementation of the policies pursued by the Union and the State Governments with respect to the minorities.
5. To look into specific complaints regarding deprivation of rights and safeguards of the minorities.
6. To suggest appropriate legal and welfare measures in respect of any minority to be undertaken by the Central or the State government.
7. To serve as a national clearing house for information in respect to the conditions of the minorities.
8. To make periodic reports at prescribed intervals to the government.

At the present time strong arguments are being made in favor of high-caste poor who are said to be ignored by the government while untouchables and other minorities are given special privileges irrespective of their economic position. These representations have found some sympathy among politicians. State governments seem to have now reduced their targets of implementing job quotas for the untouchables and the pace of providing welfare services to them. This is supposed to placate the upper-caste Hindus while maintaining compensatory privileges for untouchables.

COMPENSATORY POLICY IN THE UNITED STATES

Enormous amounts of literature were produced in the last 25 years on the status of blacks in the United States. Various analyses, conclusions and recommendations generally pointed out that the black community had yet to attain social and economic equality and effective political participation. There was no agreement whether the pace of change in the socioeconomic condition of blacks in the last two decades was reasonable in light of the hopes and expectations of this group. But American society recognized the evils of the caste system expressed through institutional racism and prepared itself to take some effective measures. More recently, political and legislative actions were taken to provide basic rights and opportunities to black people which enabled them to receive special considerations in school, housing and jobs under certain conditions.

It all began with the ruling of the U.S. Supreme Court in 1954 outlawing segregation in public schools. This was followed by the affirmative action requirement of 1961 to increase employment opportunities for racial minorities. The Civil Rights Act of 1964 prohibited exclusion of persons on the basis of race from programs and activities receiving federal financial assistance. It denied segregation in public accommodation and required effective implementation of public school desegregation and insisted on equal employment opportunities for all. The Voting Rights Act of 1965 lifted traditional barriers imposed on blacks mainly to discourage them from voter registration. An executive order in 1965 required that firms with government contracts must provide equal opportunities for minorities in their entire business operations. The federal government was also asked to do the same. The Open Housing Act of 1968 barred racial discrimination in the sale and rental of housing. The Equal Employment Opportunity Act of 1972 required that any business that employed more than 15 persons, state and local governments, and educational institutions must comply with the antidiscrimination provisions of the 1964 Civil Rights Act. It also authorized the Equal Employment Opportunity Commission to sue those employers who were engaged in discriminatory practices and empowered the courts to require specific actions by the employers to compensate for the effects of past discriminatory practices. Affirmative action was used for setting "goals" and "time tables" for employment of blacks and minority groups in occupations where they were "under-utilized." Under-utilization was defined as having fewer members of the group in the job category actually employed than would reasonably be expected from their availability. ". . . goals in this regard are nevertheless to be distinguished from quotas: while goals are required, quotas are neither required nor permitted, goals are defined as indicator(s) of probable compliance" (Goldman, 1977: 194). Employers were expected to show "good faith" in meeting numerical goals and were often pursued as if there were numerical limits beyond which they would restrict the entry of dominant groups in favor of designated minority groups. One could easily imagine affirmative action encouraging a quota system and reverse discrimination if not properly administered.

The results of more than two decades of civil rights and antipoverty programs were evaluated differently by people of different emotional and partisan persuasions. The optimists legitimately argue that the proportion of those officially listed as living in poverty was cut in half since 1959 and a significant number of blacks and other minorities were found in middle-level administrative and managerial positions and some even at the top of the income and occupational hierarchies. Blacks gained in education at all levels and their life chances improved considerably. They were still concentrated in inner-city and poor neighborhoods but more and more of them were moving into middle-income neighborhoods. What was even more significant was that most of them lived where they could afford to live. Various studies showed that the attitude of white Americans since 1970 increasingly favored racial integration, a trend which is consistent with those of the last 35 years. The factors influencing these trends were entry of larger numbers of younger persons into the population, increased education and liberal orientation on many social issues, including civil rights legislation. The difference between the Deep South and the rest of the United States also narrowed (Taylor et al., 1978: 42–44). This general movement toward liberal orientation on personal and civil liberties seemed to show a cultural change of major significance. This also reflected at least partially that the roots of individual and institutional racism—the backbone of the caste system in the United States— were being dislodged. Despite these encouraging shifts, one must remember that the caste system might still be practiced on a limited basis in certain domains reflecting consistency with the general value system of the society.

On the more pessimistic side, blacks gained only little when compared with whites. About 33 percent of all black families were still below the official poverty line. The black unemployment rate had been twice as high as white and the situation was even worse for black teenagers when compared with white teenagers. It was even more depressing that their economic position became more precarious under adverse economic conditions at the national level. Since many of them joined the labor force recently and possessed limited skills, they were more likely to be laid off during periods of economic crunch. This situation bred cynicism, uncertainty, resentment and sometimes disruption in their personal and family lives, and their participation in the community and national mainstream.

The crisis in public education has signaled difficulties for blacks in the future. Generally the poor quality of schools in the inner city, a less favorable environment for learning and ability grouping, sometimes based on prejudicial attitudes of school teachers and administrators, have subverted the concept of equality of educational opportunity (Jencks, 1972: 3-175). The social situation of blacks was different from that of whites and, therefore, various models of social mobility were less applicable to blacks. Williams (1975: 133-134) documented it as follows:

> Since 1965 there has been an outpouring of studies of social mobility, based on multivariate analysis of large data bases. Both structural and sociopsychological variables have been used in the various statistical models.... These analyses showed how greatly racial status has limited social mobility, and demonstrated that the relations of independent and intervening variables to educational and occupational attainments are different for blacks and whites.... For example, because of past discrimination many social characteristics have been less closely linked to occupation or income among blacks than among whites—e.g., local prestige or respectability, or the influence of significant others, or initial level of aspirations.

Since family background variables and race influenced the educational and occupational mobility of individuals, it was not clear what public policies would help individual blacks overcome the vicious circle of poverty and social degradation. Even if all discriminatory barriers were lifted and various institutions implemented the principle of equality of opportunity, the cumulated disabilities of the past would still hinder blacks from effectively competing for desirable positions. The compensatory measures were designed to help blacks and other minorities obtain admission to colleges and training programs. But some whites challenged such measures because they felt that these interfered with their right to equal access to opportunities. In a landmark decision in the Alan Bakke case on

June 28, 1978, the U.S. Supreme Court struck down the numerical quota set by the medical school at the University of California at Davis for members of racial minorities. But the court maintained the principles of affirmative action.

The nine justices were divided into three groups: four justices argued that the racial quota system at the University of California at Davis violated the Civil Rights Act of 1964, four ruled that race could legitimately be used in the admission policy, and finally, the one remaining, Justice Powell, agreed with the first group, arguing, however, that race could be used as a positive factor in attracting a diverse student body but candidates should still be compared on the relevant criteria for admission. Justice Powell did not agree with the argument that a racial quota would help reduce the shortage of minority doctors, or countereffect discrimination by society, because for him ''equal protection cannot mean one thing when applied to one individual and something else when applied to a person of another color'' (Newsweek, July 10, 1978: 22). He supported those against numerical quotas and joined the other group in rescuing the Affirmative Action Program. Justice Blackman, one of the four justices who defended the racial quota at Davis argued that ''. . . in order to get beyond racism, we must first take account of race. There is no other way. And in order to treat some persons equally, we must treat them differently. We cannot—we dare not—let the Equal Protection Clause perpetrate racial supremacy'' (Newsweek, July 10, 1978: 23). The diversity of opinions of these two justices reflected the deep partisan divisions within American society.

COMPENSATORY POLICY AND EQUALITY OF OPPORTUNITY

There are great difficulties for disadvantaged groups in attaining social and economic equality through the principle of equal treatment, when it is understood that talents are not equally distributed in various groups and also that there is no guarantee that the most talented will necessarily acquire higher prestige and rewards. The justification for preferential treatment depended on the ground that present disadvantages were caused by past injustices. For example, residential segregation, inferior or no education, low-paid and demeaning occupations all might have contributed to lower aspirations. Generally, most people seemed to understand these arguments as long as the preferential system did not directly interfere with the opportunities available to them. An inherent danger in preferential treatment is that "white male candidates who would have been rejected even without the policy may think they were rejected because of it, ... minority candidates who would have succeeded even without the policy may think that they have succeeded because of it. A general atmosphere develops in which it is expected that those in preferred groups will be less competent than others" (Cohen et al., 1977: xiv). These concerns have been expressed by black leaders in the United States and untouchable leaders in India and they wanted preferential systems to work effectively and accomplish the stated goals as soon as possible. It was not certain how long it would take to reach some of the goals, and this may have contributed to recent events in both the United States and India.

Our analysis of ascriptive inequality in the United States and India show that equality of opportunity, if it ever succeeded, would take a very long time to bring dramatic changes in the socioeconomic conditions of blacks and untouchables. They are poorly prepared to compete effectively and to translate equality of opportunity into equality of results. Preferential treatment, involving affirmative action in the United States and the quota system in India has helped, but they will continue to be underrepstreets. In the United States the debate whether affirmative action is effective in combating ascriptive inequalities will continue, but any hopes of a numerical quota system have vanished. It is difficult to develop effective public policy in the democratic societies that would help integrate disadvantaged groups into the mainstream, especially when resources and opportunities are perceived to be limited by the dominant groups. The traditional caste relations are on their way out but as long as blacks in the United States and the untouchables in India are not able to receive their fair share, some remnants of the caste system will continue to survive. But ascriptive inequality is becoming more and more costly, and its being cheap and functional is now open to debate.

NOTE

*Untouchables are officially as "scheduled castes" because they belong to a schedule maintained by states to determine their eligibility for compensatory privileges.

REFERENCES

Aggarwal, Pratap C. and Mohd. Siddiq Ashraf
   1976   Equality Through Privilege. New Delhi: Shri Ram Centre for Industrial Relations and Human Resources.

Berreman, Gerald D.
1960   "Caste in India and the United States." American Journal of Sociology, LXVI: 120–127.
Cohen, Marshall, Thomas Nagel and Thomas Scanlon (eds.)
1977   Equality and Educational Treatment. Princeton, N.J.: Princeton University Press
Dollard, John
1937   Caste and Class in a Southern Town. New York: Doubleday.
Duberman, Lucile
1976   Social Inequality: Caste and Class in America. Philadelphia: Lippincott C.
Dumont, Louis
1967   "Caste: A phenomenon of social structure or an aspect of Indian culture." Pp. 23–38 in Anthony de Reuck and Julie Knight (eds.), Caste and Race: Comparative Approaches. London: Churchill.
1970   Homo Hierarchicus: An Essay on the Caste System. Chicago: University of Chicago Press.
Goldman, Alan H.
1977   "Affirmative Action." Pp. 192–209 in Marshall Cohen, et al., (eds.). Equality and Preferential Treatment. Princeton, N.J.: Princeton University Press.
The Hindustan Times
1978   "Kanjhawla Arrests," September 7: 3. New Delhi: Hindustan Times Press.
Government of India
1974   India: A Reference Manual. New Delhi: Publication Division, Government of India.
Jencks, Christopher
1972   Inequality: A Reassessment of the Effect of Family and Schooling in America. New York: Basic Books.
Kemper, Theodore D.
1974   "On the nature and purpose of ascription." American Sociological Review 39: 844–853.
Mandelbaum, David G.
1970   Society in India: Change and Continuity. Berkeley: University of California Press.
Mayhew, Leon
1970   "Ascription in modern societies." Pp. 308–323 in Edward O. Laumann et al. (eds.). The Logic of Social Hierarchies. Chicago: Markham.
Newsweek
1978   "What the justices said." July 10: 22–25.
Parsons, Talcott
1964   "Evolutionary universals in society." American Sociological Review 29: 339–357.
Rosen, George
1967   Democracy and Economic Change in India. Berkeley: University of California Press.
Singh, Vijai P.
1976   Caste, Class and Democracy: Changes in a Stratification System. Cambridge, Mass.: Schenkman.
Srinivas, M. N.
1966   "A Note on Sanskritization and Westernization." Pp. 552–560 in Reinhard

Bendix and Seymour M. Lipset (eds.). Class, Status and Power: Social Stratification in Comparative Perspective. New York: Free Press.

1969   Social Change in Modern India. Berkeley: University of California Press.

Taylor, Garth D., Paul B. Sheatsley, and Andrew M. Greeley

1978   "Attitudes toward racial integration." Scientific American, 238: 42–49.

Tendulkar, D. G.

1961   Mahatma: Life of Mohandas Karamchand Gandhi, Vol. III. New Delhi: Publication Division, Government of India.

Williams, Robin M. Jr.

1975   "Race and ethnic relations." Annual Review of Sociology 1: 125–164.

STRATIFICATION IN QUEBEC SOCIETY*

JACQUES DOFNY

I

The entanglement of the Quebec economy with that of Canada and of America has been described for quite some time. One could use the language of a liberal economist or that of a Marxist to trace its contours and structures, but the facts are so obvious that they speak for themselves. In any case, the early work by Porter (1965); the statistics Raynauld and others (1968) provide; the works, inquiries and articles by Levitt (1972), Sales (1976), Milner and Milner (1973), Niosi (1978), Dubuc (1978) all confirm the same thing. To varying degrees, but following the same tendency, natural riches are granted to English or American groups. The traditional manufacturing sector, largely in the hands of English Canadians, is in a state of crisis, and its importance in the gross national product is diminishing; the American companies occupy the sectors most

Research in Race and Ethnic Relations, Volume 2, pages 115–132
Copyright © 1980 by JAI Press Inc.
All rights of reproduction in any form reserved.
ISBN: 0-89232-141-5

advanced technologically; French Canadians find themselves primarily in the nonmonopolistic sector (35 percent), and they control the establishments which employ 22.2 percent of Quebec people who receive salaries. The Quebec government has adjusted its educational and health systems to new industrial, administrative and social needs. For 20 years, it has been trying to deal with economic dependency, buying electric companies (1965) and an iron and steel industry (1964), preparing to acquire an asbestos mine and to install a factory to manufacture this product (1977), establishing a government corporation to cover a part of automobile insurance (personal risk) (1977).

There is no doubt that Quebec society is a dependent society, but what identifies it most is the fact that it is doubly dependent. Canada, in fact, has all of the characteristics of a society that is dependent on the United States. It has been during the last 10 years that the United States has made maximal efforts to purchase Canadian properties. Recently, the oil shortage has made tar sands into a profitable natural resource. The province of Alberta has a supply of 200 billion barrels of synthetic oils in Athabaska, the equivalent of a third of the oil supplies in the Middle East. A mining society has been formed in which the provinces of Alberta and Ontario together have only 25 percent of the stock; the rest is the property of Imperial Oil, Exxon, and Gulf.

Canada, then, is also a dependent society, but Quebec is doubly dependent. Economically, it depends on the United States and the rest of Canada; politically, it is part of a former British colony that is still largely dominated by English-speaking Canadians. Undoubtedly, its situation is comparable to that in Latin America for which Touraine has constructed and applied the theoretical model that he uses in *Les Sociétés Dépendantes*. The question raised by this article, as a follow-up to Touraine's reflections, is the following: In what terms and according to what model may the relations between social classes in Quebec be analyzed; how can they be defined; and how can their actions be situated within the larger field of nationalist actions and socialist actions?

In a long chapter written in 1975 on "Disarticulated societies," Touraine (1976: ch. 2) criticizes theories of dependence. He admits that these theories have advanced beyond those on modernization, formulated in the spirit of idealistic evolutionism in the nineteenth century and later revived by Redfield, Parsons, and Hozelitz. But he attributes to the dependence theories a "rigid, external determinism and a socially undetermined political voluntarism," which is another way of saying that "social behaviors should not be explained only in terms of international economic relations. . . . [It is] a position intended to challenge middle class reformers who worry about integration, nationalism, development—or in other words the 'values' which do not take social conflict into account and thereby is a position which totally is justified but which restrains the knowledge of social and political actors and therefore changes social movements into blind runners, or more precisely into actors whose actions and words do not match'' (1976: 59–60). Nonetheless, he mentions G. Frank's criticisms of the view that the modern and traditional sectors must be opposed, a view which sees the traditional sector as explainable only by virtue of its domination by the modern one.

But Touraine insists that this above all is the heart of his discussion: ''What are the relationships between the nation-state and a bourgeoisie incorporated peripherally into the international capitalist system in the development of Latin American societies?'' (1976: 65). Or elsewhere: ''The real problem that needs examining is the following: a dependent society is one whose development—or transition from one type of structure to another, and in particular from one mode of production to another—is guided directly or indirectly by a foreign bourgeoisie. How does this situation modify the fundamental social relations and in particular the social relations of production in the dependent society?'' According to Touraine, two factors should suffice to explain these characteristics: (a) the characteristic of a dependent society is the ''disarticulation'' between economic relations and the social relations within the same unit of production (synchronic analysis); (b) the ''ideal type'' is relevant for understanding both the social systems or modes of production on the one hand and the modes of development—the diachronic process—on the other.

II

The questions and hypotheses put forward by Touraine are not unrelated to some theoretical work I did many years ago (Dofny and Rioux, 1962).[1] In 1962, Carleton University in Ottawa held a colloquium to announce the upcoming publication of the book by John Porter, *Vertical Mosaic,* and empirical and theoretical attempts to describe the social structure of Canada. This work, inspired by Mills's *The Power Elite,* described the tenuous position of French Canadians in the higher strata of the major Canadian institutions: economic, political, religious, social, military, diplomatic, etc. The same situation was found everywhere: the French Canadians were underrepresented in the upper levels of all the institutions except one—the Catholic Church.

Porter placed considerable emphasis on the role the Catholic school system has played in producing more priests, lawyers, doctors and clerks than engineers, technicians, scientists or businessmen. His main hypothesis was that a fundamental difference between Canadian and American society lay in the fact that the latter had been able, under the protection and domination of White Anglo-Saxon Protestants (WASPs), to achieve a "melting pot" in which all immigrants were assimilated (an assertion that is increasingly questioned today); Canada, on the other hand, formed a vertical mosaic of ethnic groups. Porter attributed this situation to the existence of two founding societies in Canada, one English, the other French, neither of which had ever interpenetrated the other.

Mr. Rioux and I (1962) have debated the theme of "Social classes in French Canada."[2] We have maintained that one cannot use an explanation which would equate the founding groups and assume that their nonintegration served as a model for later ethnic relations. Moreover, an understanding of the values of the Catholic Church and its schools would not be sufficient to explain completely the subordinate position of French Canadians.

Assuredly, the analysis we undertook was more diachronic than synchronic. If one wishes to examine the functioning of a society, then one can study the relations between earlier classes and newly arrived ones; but if, as Touraine has said, the focus is on types of development and on how one kind of society turns another, the concepts must be different: dependence is not a mode of production but a mode of historical change; that is to say, it not only poses the question of class relations but raises as well the question of nationalism.

The notion of "ethnic class" characterizes the situation of French Canadians in Canadian and North American social structures, which structures are indistinguishable if one is analyzing the system in which French Canadians participate. In order to understand the significance of the concept of ethnic class, it is helpful to refer to the image found in the title of the Vallières book, *The White Niggers of America*. (1968). However forced it may seem, this image allows us to explore the position of French Canadians in North America. If we acknowledge Canada as an integrated part of American capitalism—to be sure, English Canadian capitalism is somewhat autonomous but is losing its importance and influence yearly—then we can compare the position of black Americans and French Canadians and determine the limits of that comparison.

In the United States, the debate concerning Blacks also proceeds from a twofold theoretical system: that of ethnic relations and that of class relations. For several more orthodox Marxists, such as Baran and Sweezy (1966), Harris (1968) or Nikolinakos (1973), ethnic stratification is only an aspect of class stratification. In order to increase the surplus value, the bourgeoisie encourages divisions between categories of workers, keeping intraclass competition at a maximum. In this same scheme, orthodox Marxists explain any social division, especially that of sex. Discussing the problem, Wilson (1974) shows that in American social history Blacks made up the marginal working class that allowed pressure to be exerted on the salaries of white workers. But he also brings up the argument from Bonacich (1972) which holds that ethnic antagonism begins in a split labor market when the price of work for the same task is different for at least two groups or would be if they performed the same work. (For Bonacich the price of work includes the cost of recruiting, transportation, lodging, education, health, and spare time activities.) In this situation, the best-paid workers, feeling threatened, oppose their competitors in ethnic terms. The best-paid group will tend to institutionalize a system of ethnic stratification that will (a) assure it a monopoly on qualified employment, (b) raise obstacles to apprenticeships and education, and (c) be opposed to legal measures that would give the competitors access to means of political pressure. From another point of view, Mandel (1955), examining American social hsitory, expressed the hypothesis that the American "labor aristocracy" could obtain high salaries to the extent that lower level tasks were left to "ethnics" and given low salaries. Wilson brings up the fact that, about 1850, the workers who were most threatened by the arrival of Blacks on the market were the Irish, who were opposed to the extension of political rights to Blacks and even succeeded in keeping them from the poorest-paying jobs. In other places, white workers who had emigrated from the South and settled in Ohio, Indiana, Illinois, adopted similar practices. According to Spero and Harris (1931: 13): "In New York City the Democratic Party . . . purported to represent the working class. It opposed the freeing of slaves on the ground that emancipation would result in the migration of thousands of Blacks to northern states, increasing competition for jobs and reducing wages even below the level to which an oversupplied labor market had already sent them." Yet other groups of workers, such as mechanics—often of Germanic origin and bearers of socialist ideas—gave their support to the abolition of slavery.

However, for Wilson, from whom this discussion is borrowed, neither orthodox Marxist theory nor the Bonacich theory can satisfactorily account for the dynamics of the conflict which set apart different categories of nineteenth-century ethnic Whites. The immigrants were ignored by the already established unions and were forced to set up their own. A fortiori, Blacks always had considerably more difficulties than had Whites in obtaining access to union organizations. Lastly, approaching the question of national liberation, Wilson quotes Lieberson, for whom "The most fundamental difference between ethnic stratification and other forms of stratification lies in the fact that the former is nearly always the basis for the internal disintegration of the existing boundaries of a nation-state. On both theoretical and empirical grounds, only ethnic groups are likely to engender a movement towards creating a separate nation-state" (1970: 173). Wilson specifically uses the example of the "Black Power Movement" in the United States and the separatist movement in Quebec. It is therefore a conjunction of class oppression and national oppression that constitutes a specific experience for certain ethnic groups and brings about behavior that cannot be explained completely by a class analysis. Thus, Wilson concludes, neither a thesis based strictly on economic determinism nor a thesis of strict ethnic antagonism which ignores class factors can account fully for reality.

French Canadians in North America are not white niggers.[3] But when they were emigrating toward the middle of the last century to textile industries in New England, they were among the "ethnics" used as cheap labor or as strike breakers (Lahne, 1944). And when American and English Canadian industry opened some firms in the second half of the nineteenth century in Quebec, it was because a wealth of cheap manual labor was to be had from this population of little peasants with large families that famine had decimated and that priests kept within the narrow confines of self-sacrifice and respect for authority. In other words, French Canadians in the North American economy made up also a split market, but they distinguished themselves from all the other "ethnics" in North America. They are a charter group, their history is not one of immigrant group gradually assimilating into a dominant group; on the contrary they are the first comers. They may have been colonized but in the course of history they were colonizers, and what colonizers! Thus their past makes them different from all other "ethnics" in North America. (Not considered, of course, are the first occupants and masters of this territory, the Indians.) They kept the flag of a glorious past, of the times when they were the conquerers of one of the biggest empires in history. (Thus, Flemish nationalism in nineteenth-century Belgium, although mainly the feat of a nation of peasants, has long since been nourished as part of the glorious past of the county of Flanders.) The second trait that distinguishes French Canadians from other "ethnics" in

North America is their concentration in one territory; they have a country and have resisted any form of assimilation. (Similarly, their Acadian cousins in Louisiana showed the same resistance to assimilation, even to the point of assimilating other Irish, German, and even Scottish immigrants [see Smith and Parenton: 1938].) In other words, if one is satisfied with a socioeconomic analysis, one can say that French Canadians are among the "ethnics" that the Anglo-Saxon American or English bourgeoisie has dominated and exploited, but they are different "ethnics" from the others. From their pre-industrial past, they have kept the memory and the traces of a merchant bourgeoisie that the English Canadian merchant class progressively eliminated. But they have always constituted a society with cultural, social, religious and administrative institutions and a bourgeoisie of merchants, lawyers, clerks, doctors, judges, deputies, ministers, canons, bishops, and cardinals.

Even more, they have always had a societal plan which is contrary to plans for their assimilation. For the Crown of London, it was a matter of integrating and assimilating (British North American Act) this nation of 600,000 small peasants and its limited segment of bourgeois merchants, notaries and lawyers, enclosed by the Church. The patriots revolted in 1837–1838 and were hanged. But if political and economic integration was realized, sociological integration never succeeded. The social (and clerical) French Canadian structure remained. For many historians, the division between economic and cultural influences occurred between the French Canadian Church and British power, each one therein finding its wealth.

But it is easy to understand that when big industry—steel, railroads, automobiles, chemistry and electronics—develops, it is an entirely different bourgeoisie which takes over, exploits natural resources, and in a word owns or at least controls nearly all of economic life. From this great capitalist bourgeoisie, French Canadians are excluded. Readily noted are some conquering entrepreneurs at the beginning of the century whose empire subsequently has disappeared, or some more recent entrepeneus whose empires seem just as ephemeral or is now closely integrated into the English Canadian banking system. There have always been entrepeneurs in Quebec, but ever since the beginning of industrial society there has never been a class of French Canadian capitalists who own the natural wealth and the means for transforming the country, a class equivalent to that which Marx described for England and France. In terms of "non-owners of the means of production" one can refer to the French Canadians as a dominated class and the English bourgeoisie of

Quebec and Canada as a whole as a dominating class. These two classes can be described, it seems to me, as ethnics.

III

Historically, there has existed a particular North American industrial economic structure. It had its origins in the eastern zone of the continent (symbol: railroads), resulted in more recent developments of the West and the South (symbol: aviation) and evolved at the beginning of the century through the high industrialization found around the Great Lakes (symbol: automobile). In these three periods, the Quebec economy provided the natural resources necessary for development: wood, iron, aluminum, asbestos and electricity, for the most part. (Typically, the weakest part of the economic structure of contemporary Quebec is the transformational sector; even in this sector the older labor-intensive industries are very important. Thus, Quebec is very much affected by transfer to the periphery.)

During this evolution—from World War One on but especially after World War Two—American capital gradually has been replacing English Canadian capital. The distributions in the primary, secondary and tertiary sectors tend to be comparable in Quebec, Canada, and the United States. There has been an expansion of the middle classes, a progressive diminution of farmers, a reduction in blue-collar workers and an increase in white-collar workers. Special attention has been given to the role and composition of the old and the new middle classes, in which one finds small businessmen, managing directors of cooperatives, teachers, journalists, tradesmen and all the new categories of technicians which modern industry and the "social affairs" that accompany it recruit and train. This petty bourgeoisie has been discussed and analyzed at length. The importance of the new petty bourgeoisie in the ranks of the separatist party has been noted. It is true that Quebec has a provincial government which allocates two-thirds of its budget to the sectors of education and health. Successive governments have been preoccupied with these problems and have achieved notable reforms that big firms could only regard favorably. These governments were supported in their efforts by an electorate who abandoned the old National Union Party for the modernizing Liberal Party.

In such a situation, class allegiances are not easily identifiable; the absence of a party representing the working class illustrates this situation. The stakes most important for the working class are not brought up at the time of provincial elections. In this sense, Quebec union organizaitons have a political role that is unusual in industrially advanced societies. Clearly, there is a separation between the economic and social aspects: "Class groups are opposed to each other in terms of their varying relationships to the system of domination" which is foreign (Touraine, 1976: 99). The situation resembles the Touraine analysis of social classes in a dependent society. Speaking of Latin America, he notes that "the words most often used are not those of the *proletariat* and the *bourgeoisie,* but those of the *people* and of *oligarchy.* They must be defined. The most explicit and easily understood is *pueblo. This word indicates the coincidence of a category that is communal, national, regional or local* [emphasis added]. That is to say, in this word the elements of *ascription* are more important than are those of *achievement."* Furthermore, "In Latin America, the people represent both a class and a local or regional reality violated by foreign penetration" (1976: 102). "A dependent society is divided into two with the separation of a privileged sector tied to foreign interests from a popular national sector that is marginal, repressed, or simply underprivileged" (1976: 105).

Of Quebec, one could say that the society is split into three parts, given that two foreign interests prevail: English Canadian and those of the United States. As for the Quebec government, it has expanded considerably since 1960. Its technocratic and bureaucratic machinery has swelled to such a point that it has become the largest employer. This happens to coincide with a system of collective bargaining devised for isolated production units and not for entire professional sectors such as hospitals or educational institutions. It has become an entrepreneur but of a public service—by nationalizing electrical utilities or acquiring steelworks. The Quebec Party, now in power, is striving to push nationalist demands as far as possible within the limits of parliamentary democracy. Although at first it represented itself as radically for independence and moderately social-democratic, the Party altered its pretensions when it acceded to power. Its militants are enlisted from a fraction of the industrial and commercial petty bourgeoisie, from among the liberal professionals, the civil servants, the engineers, technicians, white-collar workers from the private and public sectors, and a minority of blue-collar workers. The members of government are primarily from the universities.

Polls taken shortly before the last election showed 50–60 percent of the workers in favor of the Quebec Party. Admittedly, the victory of the Quebec Party was interpreted more as a protest vote, brought about by the serious economic crisis which has been raging for several years. The same polls indicated that the separatist option itself would attract only

24–28 percent of the voters. Undoubtedly, the Party has popular support—it could be called "populist"—directed primarily by a Christian-democratic intelligentsia and former higher-level civil servants.

In effect, the bourgeoisie (in the broadest sense of the word) is not to be found in the Party ranks, since the bourgeoisie is almost entirely American or English Canadian. Nor is it mostly a working class party. During the period preceding the election, unions did not hide their sympathy for the Quebec Party, but two out of three central unions kept their distance from the government, although the Quebec Federation of Labor, a liaison office for most of the federations affiliated with the American Federation of Labor/Congress of Industrial Organizations (AFL-CIO), openly supports the government since it has come to power. As for the Confederation des Syndicats Nationaux (CSN) much more sensitive to socialist currents, it announced at the time of its Congress in June 1978 that it favored a socialist society, criticized the "sovereignty association" option of the government as ambiguous, and rejected the creation of a socialist party as being outside its responsibility, but recognized the need for giving workers the training that woudl allow them to effectuate a socialist project. The third union, that of the teachers, was just as critical of the Quebec Party, and it too hopes for a society built for and by workers.

One can see in Quebec those characteristics which Touraine has attributed to dependent societies. The working class, part of the national community, is not disinterested in the national question, nor can it be. But the labor organizations which represent the working class cannot leave the matter to professionals nor can they afford to support a national project which does not provide adequate quarantees to defend its interests nor a satisfactory vision of a society to which workers could ascribe. As for the employers, they are just as cautious; it is no secret that American business and government hope to keep the Canadian market, including Quebec, organized on a federal basis. Moreover, if the Quebec Party succeeded without any manifest political or military risks in having Quebec separate, there could be risks in the long run if the independent Quebec began to turn to socialism. Seeing a new Cuba suddenly appear so near to New York and Washington is unthinkable.

IV

The analysis of classes and class relations in Quebec necessitates the use of a twofold system of stratification. At the first level of analysis, one can describe the situation of French Canadians as similar to that of the "ethnics" of North America, dominated by the capitalism of White

Anglo-Saxon Protestants. But these same French Canadians belong to another truncated system of stratification if the level of analysis is the province of Quebec. In fact, French Canadians coexist with English Canadians (10 percent) and immigrants (10 percent). If one uses the notion of class to identify behavior and attitudes, either political, religious, economic or sexual, there is not much chance for treating these three groups as if they belonged to the same society, to the same class system. One must accept the fact that there are two social structures, based as much on social and political history as on economic structures. As for the immigrants, although they have their own subculture, they tend to integrate into the professional and economic (and above all educational) life of the dominant structure. Likewise, it has often been argued that, in contrast to an analysis based on a dual structure, one finds in Quebec French Canadian capitalists, on the one hand, and on the other English Canadian workers with whom the French Canadian workers share common class membership. As for the French Canadian entrepreneurs, it is a known fact that they are concentrated in the sectors of small and medium-sized firms, whether they supply local labor markets or function as satellites of monopolistic enterprises. English Canadian blue-collar workers number approximately 50,000,[4] such a slight fraction that one cannot regard them as important in the Quebec class system. When it has been a matter of debating the destiny of the Quebec community, the English Canadian workers from Quebec and from the rest of Canada have never manifested a great solidarity with the lot of the French Canadian workers. In the labor assemblies of Quebec, the workers had the right to express themselves in English, but the French Canadians who live and work in Ontario have not had the right to use French.

It is impossible to study French Canadians, wherever they are found in North America, in Canada, or in Quebec, without using a pluralistic system of stratification and class relations. In the same way, certain authors have spoken about an external bourgeoisie, an inner bourgeoisie, and a comprador bourgeoisie, using three concepts to describe the bourgeoisie. It is clear that the internal bourgeoisie maintains a system of class relations. It has a certain type of relationship with the external bourgeoisie and with the internal working class. Likewise, the internal working class has a certain type of relationship with the internal bourgeoisie depending on the historic community to which they both belong. But they have other sorts of relationships to the external working class for the community, even if these relationships are often—but not necessarily—relationships of alliance, similar to the competitive alliances that the members of the bourgeoisie maintain among themselves.

The student of Quebec society continually encounters this disjunction, this parallelism or this combination of class relations. The historical society is always there like a volcano that is not entirely extinct and that at a particular juncture again becomes active. The first Quebec Party Congress, after the big victory in 1976, gathered only a couple of hundred militants; the charismatic Congress, a few weeks later, brought together 50,000 of them. The Old Stories of the Upland, a novel written and broadcast over the radio before the Second World War—a story about poor peasants at the start of the century—continues today to attract record audiences. The Quebec Party, shortly after assuming power, erected before the Quebec Parliament a statue of Duplessis, incarnation of the old and spurned regime. Square dancers and fiddlers vie for radio time with Charlebois and Quebec "disco." It could even be suggested that the recent elevation of Claude Ryan to the leadership of the Liberal Party, after having served as secretary for the commission of bishops for 20 years and later as director of Le Devoir,[5] symbolizes the return of traditional Catholic forces, always supporters of the old pact between the English government and the Catholic Church. Recent polls (June 1978) show the popularity of this type of social leader. It would be erroneous to classify Claude Ryan as the "representative of big capitalism." The big capitalists are physically absent, but they have their representatives, managers, and directors. It is not possible to confuse the manager of the General Motors plant at Sainte-Therese with the general director of General Motors in Detroit, nor with the board of directors of this multinational. But their delegate is present in the Council of Quebec employers.

There are certain class relationships that derive from the earlier social system, as is evident when journalists go on strike against a French Canadian daily like Le Devoir. In such a case, class relations are characterized by the social actors involved. It should be remembered, however, that the mode of relations (the legal type of collective bargaining) and the content of the negotiation (salaries or grievance rights) are borrowed from modes of collective bargaining practiced throughout the American continent. Similarly, a federation affiliated with AFL-CIO can guide a negotiation with a small French Canadian entrepreneur while simultaneously undertaking bargaining with one of the largest multinational manufacturers of nickel. In both cases, the adversaries of the union are not parts of the same economic market, one having a distinctly regional character and the other, a distinctly international one. The international division of work sometimes splits economic units in which the market, the labor force, and the society coincide. In other cases, found more and more frequently, the coincidences no longer exist, and if the management of multinational firms succeeds in perfecting their economic or social strategies, this rarely is the case with the labor force which is more closely tied to the interests and conditions of each national society.

Political class relationships also come into play in many settings and also tend toward disjointedness, parallelism and combinations. The separation of provincial from federal elections is perfectly clear institutionally. One can often find in political history this duality, corresponding to the twofold system of stratification. One can at the same time favor a very nationalist government in Quebec and a very federalistic government in Ottawa. That is to say, one can play simultaneously different games on different chessboards. Even if it is the same people who behave in this way, they are not politically schizophrenic but are playing different roles in different societies. Certainly, if one wants to change this situation and abolish one of the chessboards, a certain type of political class relations will disappear. But the structures are intertwined and have been so for some time, any effort to dissociate them is difficult and is accompanied by promises and hopes ultimately for "mending." In other words, what is separated is only to be joined back together in a different way, a way more adapted to the changes which have taken place in the social structure of Quebec and of North American capitalism. In the same way, certain union federations affiliated with the AFL-CIO would not mind leaving the Canadian federated league and reporting to the head office in Detroit or Pittsburgh; additionally, French Canadian brokerage houses wish to negotiate loans directly with Wall Street without the use of English Canadian intermediaries. And in the same way, a Quebec socialist party would not deem it necessary to become only a branch of the English Canadian New Democratic Party, even if it were inclined to reach an agreement about elections with this party.

V

As can be seen, class relations are both conjoined and disjoined: actors can behave identically in different stratification systems or in different, even contradictory, ways. They can be mobilized at different times or at the same time over conflicts or strategies whose stakes depend either on class struggle or historical change. But class struggle always accompanies historical change; the intensity will depend on historical developments or social conflicts. When at the time of the Second World War the majority of French Canadians refused conscription, they appealed more to a national conscience than to a class conscience. The difference was not that between the worker, the lawyer or the French Canadian entrepreneur, but that between ''the'' French Canadians and ''the'' English Canadians. If on the other hand the government in Ottawa made important technological changes in Canadian post offices, resistance would occur in all post offices in Canada; often the French Canadian postal employees are the most combative and the last to return to work. In contrast, in certain conflicts pitting Quebec workers against the Quebec government, it has often been the workers in the English hospitals who triggered the struggle or who pursued it for the longest time.

Thus, depending on the stakes, different structural mechanisms are set in motion. The stakes can depend on relationships of production or on historical change. The mechanisms can be so interconnected as some pawns move forward others simultaneously or at the wrong time advance in different ways on different economic, social, and political spaces.

A class analysis demands that one never lose sight of the fact that a system of class relations can be embedded in a larger system dominated by the social forces of another society. But national systems themselves result from different stratification systems at different phases of development. Thus, one can still recognize in France vestiges of nobility, the dominant class in the fuedal system. One can still see an important category of large landowners and a corresponding category of agricultural workers. Even if the role of these categories remains important, it is attacked by the dominant forces in subsequent phases of capitalism, as occurs with the development of multinational agribusiness. Whatever alliance can be forged between forces born of different systems, as one phase of capitalism merges into another the typology of the principal actors is no longer the same.

The nobility left Quebec at the time of the English conquest. What remained was a nation of little peasants and their parish priests, notaries, lawyers, and merchants. This small nation was unable to accumulate the resources necessary to set capitalism in motion, or if it sometimes tried to do so, it was quickly thwarted by its conquerors and not encouraged by the clergy. This nation of little farmers has been transformed over the past hundred years into a nation of industrial workers. But they have had neither the means for economic accumulation nor for social accumulation. There are few social heirs in Quebec. Social dynasties are unfamiliar, and those which do exist are recent. Thus, superimposed on a class system with few large landowners and an array of small independent farmers (hence differing greatly from dependent societies in Latin America and the situation of blacks in North America) is an industrial society whose dominant class had always been foreign. The petty bourgeoisie—of which certain of its actions bring to mind the black American bourgeoisie, notably the long resistance to unionism or the attempt to develop Catholic union shops at the beginning of the century[6]—constantly has played the part of an auxiliary, a subcontractor, a manager of English Canadian and American capitalism. To this middle class, born of industrialization, is added a class which is becoming more and more important and entrusted with the affairs of the provincial government, technocratic or bureaucratic. Its importance, no matter how large it may seem in the political process, should not obscure the fact that the provincial government itself often acts as if it were the manager of the social affairs of one of the sectors of the North American market. It is not from this class that a social movement could be born. If a social movement is to launch a plan for French Canadians, it can come only from the working class, sole heir of the original settlers of the country.

This new class is not a nineteenth-century working class, corresponding to nineteenth-century capitalism; it is a conglomeration of professional categories,[7] the locus of most contemporary industrial employment, the result of the diversification of tasks produced over two centuries by the mechanical division of labor. These professional categories are grouped into families according to the particular industrial branch, or according to new scientific disciplines, or according to their applications. Between the numerous occupations which fit together are points of contact; minor changes or deliberate actions move sectors from one family to another, from one status to another, and from one hierarchical rank to another. The heterogeneity of the socio-professional stratum is great; one cannot readily place a fitter craftsman, a nurse, a managing secretary, a ministry's statistician, a female laboratory assistant and a truck driver into the same social class. If they find themselves in union federations or confederations their employment and working conditions are so different that communal action proves difficult. Furthermore, in general they begin to understand that their working conditions depend on mechanisms of power, the contours of which they come to recognize. The cohesion which cannot be attained at the professional level is achieved at the level of the employment sector, the region, the community, or the national collectivity. The dynamic set in motion by interaction of classes and nationalities will be found at the interface of professional cleavages which increasingly acquire regional or national aspects.

It would be wrong to attribute the phenomenon of multiple stratification and systems of power relations only to dependent societies. The oldest industrial societies all were found on ethnic, religious, and national divisions. Polish miners from the Ruhr went on strike in the second half of the nineteenth century with their flag out front. Irish workers in the steelworks of Sheffield communicated during the feast-day of Saint Patrick and waited for the liberation of their native country. Flemish miners of Wallonie had to learn Walloon at the beginning of the century to take orders from Walloon foremen (later they worked more often at the surface of the mine and the Poles, then the Italians and Greeks, took orders from the sons of the Flemish miners). "Croquant" is still spoken in certain workshops and farms in Occitania (South France); French or "joual" is spoken among workers in Montreal.

Each stratum in a society is itself a fragment, made up of subunits which vary in age, in vitality, in social vigor. An analysis of contemporary society which focuses only on class relations cannot be profound. It is equivalent to the situation in which a botanist would cut through the stem of a plant and then describe its various parts, systems, horizontal canals. Such would be purely a synchronic view of social phenomena. But one must analyze as well the vertical structures which respond to major movements, to past developments, to historical change; it is the superimposition of these two levels of analysis that permits us to understand the dynamics of social life.

Quebec and Canada are encountering one of these moments, one of the historical turning points. The British Canadians seek to affirm their autonomy while holding on to a symbol, the British crown; the French Canadians seek their own autonomy but busily brandish the fleur-de-lis flag of independence. But in both cases, it means fundamentally a disengagement from British imperial structures and an attracion towards (and by) the very powerful American empire. At the moment when this historical movement is taking place, social classes constitute the complex and ramified entities described above. They coincide with an ethnic cleavage that makes Quebec a dependent society in a federal government which itself is dependent.

NOTES

*Originally published as "Les stratifications de la société québécoise" in *Sociologie et Sociétés* 10 (October, 1978):87–102. Translated by Nancy C. Holden, University of Wisconsin-Madison.
    1. The work has been criticized many times, notably by Laurin and Bourque (1970); Halary (1978); Roussopoulos (1972); and Rocher (1962). I am taking this occasion to clarify my ideas on the issue. See also Arnaud and Dofny (1977).

2. Later, Rioux in his manner pursued the issue in an article which appeared in 1965 in Recherches Sociographiques. In the controversy which ensued, both versions were used interchangeably.

3. It must be noted, however, that of all the ethnic groups in the United States, blacks—by virtue of their numbers, their concentration in the South, their slave status— have come closest to representing a separate society; it is in fact the only group which has made a nationalist claim.

4. Of these blue-collar workers 17.3 percent are "specialists and semispecialists," although this category constitutes 25.3 percent of the entire blue-collar labor force in Quebec. For a discussion on the English working class aristocracy see M. Van Schendel, "Les classes ouvrières faibles. Le cas québécois," Contradiction 3, 1973.

5. Le Devoir was founded in 1910 by Henri Bourassa, a famous nationalist/journalist. This journal has been oriented to a clientele of intellectuals and prints 55,000 copies. In the past, the archbishop assumed the deficits.

6. "It is a lamentable fact, well known to all organizers who have worked in industries employing considerable numbers of Negroes, that there is a large and influential black leadership including ministers, politicians, editors, doctors, lawyers, social workers, etc., who as a matter of race tactics are violently opposed to their people going into the trade union." William Z. Foster, The Great Steel Strike and its Lessons, New York: Huebsch, 1920 (cited in Bonacich, 1976).

7. Their average income places them, on an international scale, in the highest bracket.

REFERENCES

Arnaud, N., and Dofny, J.
1977 Nationalism and the National Question. Montréal. Black Rose Books.
Baran, P. A. and Sweezy, P. M.
1966 Monopoly Capital. New York: Monthly Review Press.
Bonacich, Edna
1972 "A theory of ethnic antagonism: the split labor market." American Journal of Sociology 37: 547–559.
Bonacich, Edna
1976 "Advanced capitalism and black-white relations." American Sociological Review 41.
Dofny, Jacques and Marcel Rioux
1962 "Les classes sociales au Canada francais." Review Francaise de Sociologie 3: 290–300.
Dubuc. A.
1978 "Les fondements historiques de la crise des sociétés canadienne et québécoise." Politique Aujourd'hui: 7–8.
Halary, C.
1978 "Le débat sur les relations entre conscience de classe et conscience nationale au Québec, 1960–1976." Anthroplolgie et Sociétés. Québec: Presses Université Laval.
Harris, N.
1968 "Race and nation." International Socialism 34: 2226.

Lahne, Herbert J.
1944   The Cotton Mill Worker. New York: Farrar and Rinehart.
Laurin, N. and Bourque, G.
1970   "Classes sociales et idéologies nationalistes au Québec." Socialisme Québécois 20.
Levitt, K.
1972   La Capitulation Tranquille. Montréal: L'Étincelle.
Lieberson, Stanley
1970   "Stratification and ethnic groups." Sociological Inquiry 40:172–181.
Mandel, Bernard
1955   Labor: Free and Slave Workingmen and the Anti-Slavery Movement in the United States. New York: Associated Authors.
Milner, S. and Milner, H.
1973   The Décolonization of Quebéc. Toronto: McClelland and Stewart.
Nicolinakos, M.
1973   "Notes on an economic theory of racism." A Journal of Race and Intergroup Relations: 14.
Niosi, J.
1978   Le Contrôle Financier du Capital Canadien. Montréal: Presses de l'üniversité du Québec.
Porter, John H.
1965   The Vertical Mosaic. Toronto: The University of Toronto Press.
Raynauld, A., Marion, G. and Béland, R.
1968   La Répartition des Revenus Entre Les Groupes Ethniques du Canada. Rapport de la Commission d'enquête sur le bilinguisme et biculturalisme.
Rocher, Guy
1962   "Les recherches sur les occupations et la stratification sociale." Recherches Sociographiques 3: 173–184.
Roussopoulos, D.
1972   "Nationalism and social classes in Quebec." Our Generation 8.
Sales, A.
1976   Capital, Enterprise et Bourgeoisie. Thèse de doctorat d'État, Université de Paris.
Smith, T. L. and Parenton, V. J.
1938   "Acculturation among the Louisiana French." American Journal of Sociology 44: 355–364.
Spero, S. D. and Harris, A. L.
1931   The Black Worker: The Negro and the Labor Movement. New York: Columbia University Press.
Touraine, A.
1976   Les Sociétés Dépendentes. Paris: Gembloux.
Vallières, Pierre
1971   White Niggers of America: The Precocious Autobiography of a Quebec Terrorist. Montreal. Ed. Parti-Pris.
Wilson, W. J.
1974   "Ethnic and class stratification: their interrelation and political consequences." Paper delivered at the Eighth World Congress of Sociology, Toronto.

SOCIAL STRUCTURE AS METATHEORY:
IMPLICATIONS FOR RACE RELATIONS THEORY AND RESEARCH

DARNELL F. HAWKINS

INTRODUCTION

As several observers have noted (Gordon, 1965; Baratz and Baratz, 1970; Valentine, 1968; Ryan, 1971; Williams, 1970), during the 1960s there was a convergence in American social science research and theory on what has been called "cultural deprivation." This term was—and still is—used widely to explain the differential performance of American public school children. Numerous studies undertaken in the 1950s and 1960s documented differences between various economic and cultural groups.

Gordon provides a thorough summary of the studies on cultural depri-

Research in Race and Ethnic Relations, Volume 2, pages 133–150
Copyright © 1980 by JAI Press Inc.
All rights of reproduction in any form reserved.
ISBN: 0-89232-141-5

vation published before 1964. He points out that investigators tended to focus on several features of culturally deprived children: (1) their family status, (2) their language, cognition and intelligence, (3) their perceptual style and patterns of intellectual functioning, and (4) their motives and aspirations. The children generally considered to be culturally deprived were the children of the lower class, including many poor whites, and certain American racial and ethnic minorities, especially blacks, native Americans, Puerto Ricans, and Chicanos.

As Gordon indicates, the research studies primarily have enumerated various pathological characteristics of the so-called deprived. Critics suggest that most of the theories and data use the white, middle-class American child as the criterion. The deprived child who is thought to depart from certain norms is regarded as deficient. Often the norms are unexamined. For example, culturally deprived children are said to lack the ability to defer gratification. Yet, seldom do researchers show the extent to which deferred gratification is valued or common among middle-class children. Thus, the deficit model explains the poor educational performance of some children on the basis of assumed social inadequacies. Ryan argues that such a model "blames the victim," since it does not examine structural bases of unequal educational achievement (see also Baratz and Baratz, 1970).

Why has this model or paradigm prevailed in social science research on educational performance? One explanation could be that it is firmly supported by research. Proponents point to the mass of empirical studies which document the problems of low income and minority youth. Indeed, the extensiveness of research conducted by sociologists, psychologists, linguists, educators and others might seem to prove cultural deficiency. But opponents of deprivation theory challenge this explanation. They point to the inadequacies in much of the extant research and call attention to the ideological biases in analyses. The present paper elaborates on this viewpoint. It is my contention that the deficit model is not entirely empirically derived; it is not merely the product of theory testing. Instead, it is based at least partly on ccrtain metatheoretical assumptions in the social sciences about the nature of the social structure.

My purpose here is to demonstrate that cultural deprivation theory, especially as applied to black Americans, has resulted from a kind of conceptual leap by researchers at the metatheoretical level of analysis. This leap, more than empirical tests and proof at the level of substantive theory and research, provides the grounding for deprivation theory. In this respect, the theory can be regarded as being ideologically founded.

The willingness of researchers to make the leap may be influenced by a variety of ideological and structural forces operating in American social science and in American society.

In summary, my aim is to show that many of the problems associated with cultural deprivation theorizing stem rather directly from the preeminence structural approaches hold. To make this argument, I examine first the use of the term "social structure." Next, I review the work on cultural deprivation. Finally, I consider the analyses on deprivation in the context of structural analyses "in the social sciences".

ON THE MEANING OF SOCIAL STRUCTURE

Most sociologists accept the idea that each society is structured, although different investigators may emphasize different aspects of that structure. What at the most general level do scholars mean by social structure? Homans (1975: 53) points out that for most, the concept captures "those aspects of social behavior that the investigator considers relatively enduring and persistent." Different investigators may debate the exact nature and form of these behaviors and their relative persistence, but they accept the idea that there is some uniformity in society.

Some observers focus on aspects of behavior thought to be long-lasting. Those aspects would include formal organizations, institutions which are not organizations, and patterns of interaction among members of a small group. Used in this sense, structure can be thought of as any patterned, persisting set of social roles.

Other researchers stress those features regarded as fundamental in any society. For example, some treat economic phenomena as more determinative of social life than are other phenomena. From this perspective, structural characteristics are those which are basic in a social system. Finally, sociologists use the term to denote an entity which is divisible—at least conceptually—but in which the parts are interconnected. These, then, are the most common uses of the term (also see Goode, 1975). For the purposes of this analysis, I am interested in the use of the term "social structure" to describe a system of interrelated parts.

Homans (1975: 55) makes the comment that for sociologists "the interdependence of parts is just what maintains the relative persistence, or equilibrium, of the structure; the interrelations of the parts with one another dampens the variation that is possible in any one of them." The emphasis on interdependence presents difficulties. At its worst, it can lead to a crude structural determinism, such as is evident in pseudo-evolutionary approaches to the theory of modernization. Those approaches treat changes in the family, kinship patterns, law, religion and other phases of social life as inevitable products of political and economic modernization. Aside from an ethnocentric bias which holds that all modernizing societies will come to resemble the United States or Europe, the approaches place too great an emphasis on the idea that variation and change in one part will alter all parts. The approaches take for granted the idea that one can predict change based on certain earlier modifications (see Coser, 1975, for a critique of this theme).

For most sociologists the concept of social structure is basic; most accept the notion that a society embodies a structure. The widespread use of the term may obscure problems. First, its frequent use may suggest that there is consensus among researchers on its meaning. We may be misled into assuming that because the term is employed so often, all of its users have in mind the same theoretical framework. Second—and more importantly for this discussion—the adoption of the concept could inhibit empirical inquiry. If one believes that any social structure has particular properties and consequences, he might see little reason for studying all aspects of a given society.

ON CULTURAL DEPRIVATION THEORY

Williams (1970: 1-3) argues that one of the key concepts developed during the 1960s was the idea that the boundaries of poverty often are subcultural ones. Some would trace the contention to the work by Lewis (1959). Lewis, an anthropologist, used the term "culture of poverty" to describe the cultural aspects of economically impoverished societies. He sought to distinguish between culture and poverty but attributed certain aspects of disorganization in subcultures of Western societies to the impact of systematic, historical poverty. His ideas are similar to those of the Chicago school of sociologists who stressed the disorganizing effects of poverty in American urban areas.

Much of the work of educators and other social scientists who have provided the bulk of empirical studies on cultural deprivation do not appear to have been guided specifically by the Lewis analysis, however. In fact, as Baratz (1969: 94) has remarked, Lewis and other anthropologists would not describe a people as deprived or devoid of culture. Thus, to understand the popularity of cultural deprivation theory, we must look beyond the work from Lewis.

Cultural deprivation theory could be the result of either of two processes. First, it might have arisen from certain ideological-political trends and values in the larger American society. Such values could have penetrated social science through the values of individual researchers as well as through certain organizational or structural features of modern society. The Baratzes, among others, have called attention to the fact that the decade of the 1960s was typified by greater governmental use of social science theory and research to solve economic and social problems. Thus, accompanying and reinforcing the proliferation of social research was a governmental policy focused on reform and social change. But cultural deprivation theory might be the product of accumulated empirical research and empirically based concepts whose formulation has been guided by scientific inquiry. In other words, the prominence of the theory could result from its proven explanatory power.

Ideological Bases of Deprivation Theory

Is the widespread application of a deficit model attributable to the institutional racism and class orientation of a predominantly white middle-class establishment? Several observers have made this charge. Baratz (1969; also see Baratz and Baratz, 1970) and the Valentines (1975) are among the commentators who have outlined ideological issues in the use of deprivation theory. The issues are somewhat varied. First, as the above question implies, one could treat deficit theorizing as the outcome of political struggles which pit white against black, middle-income groups against low-income ones. But deprivation models might also gain the support of both blacks and whites because such models coincide with particular orientations. Third, the emphasis on cultural deprivation could be linked to disciplinary developments in which different paradigms compete for ascendancy (see Kuhn, 1970, for a discussion of paradigms in scientific inquiry). Running throughout the discussion presented below is the theme that cultural deprivation theory may be a focal point through which ideological concerns are funneled into social scientific research.

Baratz (1969) begins by noting the way in which linguists, educators, and psychologists have offered three different assessments of the linguistic abilities of black children, and the relationship of such abilities to educational performance. Baratz and Baratz (1970) argue that programs of early childhood intervention based on notions of deficit represent a form of institutionalized racism, buttressed and supported by social science research. Ryan (1971:7) concludes that deficit theorizing "is a brilliant ideology for justifying a perverse form of social action designed not to change society, as one might expect, but rather society's victim."

Gouldner (1970) and Taylor et al. (1974:22–25) suggest that cultural deprivation theory is the product of a liberal sociology, a utilitarian inspired sociology linked with political efforts to produce a meritocratic society without attacking the larger, structural-institutional bases of inequality. The "cultural deprivation" inspired educational programs of the 1960s are thus seen as part of a larger political effort to "attack deprivation" in all its forms (Taylor et al., 1975:12).

The appeal and subsequent widespread use of cultural deprivation theorizing and conceptualizing are seen as the result of an affinity with certain larger political-ideological trends and values. For example, cultural deprivation theory offers an environmental explanation for the educational deficits of those labeled "deprived." As such, it provides a counterpoint to the genetic and pseudo-genetic conceptions of deprivation which have underlain so much of earlier, social Darwinist influenced social science (e.g., see Hofstadter, 1944). In cultural deprivation theory human beings are seen as malleable and changeable. Change can be induced.

Because of its focus on external conditions, cultural deprivation theory has found proponents among liberal social scientists and even among some minority group scholars who accept the idea of deficiencies but who seek nongenetic explanations (e.g., see the work of Frazier, 1932, 1949, 1968). Further, this is a theory which stresses the importance of remediation and social reform in the struggle to eradicate deprivation. Thus, it appeals to activist sentiments.

At one level of analysis, one might attribute the popularity of a deficit model to institutional racism and economic inequality (see Baratz and Baratz, 1970; Blauner, 1972; Gouldner, 1970). Control over the sources of scholarly research and publication, training of students, setting of professional standards could serve to enhance the interests of a predominantly white, middle-class social science establishment. Such an analysis suggests that increased professionalism promotes the ascendancy of particular paradigms and, in this instance, of a specific model. Others have stressed the impact of governmental control of the direction of research through the selective channeling of research funding. All of this concentrates on the various institutional means for the funneling of definite ideologies into social science research.

What are the mechanisms by which these larger societal assumptions and values are transformed into social science concepts? What factors other than ideology may explain the seeming predominance of this form of theorizing? What is the role of empirical research in the acceptance of particular paradigms? These broader issues are examined in the context of cultural deprivation theory. I give considerable attention to questions of ideology but review in the next section the argument that deprivation theory in fact may be nonideologically based.

Nonideological Bases of Deprivation Theory

In contrast to the ideological focus taken to the analysis of cultural deprivation theory, proponents have chosen to emphasize the nonideological basis for the ascendancy of the concept. In this regard, Taylor et al. (1974: 31) suggest that: "Two types of questions can be asked of any theory: what is its explanatory power, and what is its appeal?" A part of the appeal of cultural deprivation theory rests on its ideological stance, but what of its explanatory power?

The authors raise an important issue, but they appear to make far too clear-cut a distinction between explanatory power and appeal. A theory with great explanatory power (or perceived explanatory power) often has great appeal by virtue of that fact alone. There is also an ideological commitment among social scientists, and all scientists, to certain scientific canons, rules and procedures. Among these are certain ideas regarding the validity and reliability of theoretical approaches. These scientific values and commitments are judged necessary within the community of scientists.

Thus, social science may be viewed as being influenced by a collective commitment by researchers to certain scientific rules and procedures for conducting research and for proving theories. Theory building ideally is guided by these rules and involves a constant process of formulation, testing and reformulation. The methodological limitations of much of the research on the deficit model would seem to indicate that the model was not developed by this procedure. As will be elaborated on in the next section, the data base for deprivation theory is not nearly as well developed as one might assume, given the popularity of the theory.

CULTURAL DEPRIVATION AND SOCIAL STRUCTURAL ANALYSIS

An abundant literature details shortcomings of deprivation theory. In the area of family research, several recent studies challenge earlier perspectives on the nature of black family life. Those perspectives linked economic deprivation to family disorganization, with female-headed households used as an indicator of disorganization. The argument held that a vicious cycle occurred, in which family problems underscored economic disadvantage and were in turn the products of that disadvantage.

Billingsley (1968), Hill (1971), Scanzoni (1971), and Allen (1978) offer an alternative view. They argue that black and poor families should not be judged according to the normative standards applied to white middle-class families; that the use of these standards has led to the deficit view. These observers contend, too, that many of the conclusions in the literature were not based on extensive empirical research on black families. Rather, the generalizations seem to have been based on ideological and normative considerations.

Other challenges are made on methodological and empirical grounds.

For example, Miller (1964) warns against assuming homogeneity in large populations classified as lower class and disadvantaged. Earlier Dave (1963) and Riessman (1962) proposed and attempted to show that the parents of the deprived child could provide stimulating learning environments in the home. More recently, Ginsburg (1972) and Keddie (1973), amassing a diversity of studies and findings, have denounced as a dangerous myth the notion of cultural deprivation.

These findings and others offer evidence that counter findings of deficit in the home environment, intellect and cognitive functioning and language of the deprived child. Other studies suggest that even if differences between those children labeled "deprived" and those labeled "non-deprived" are shown to exist, no empirical link has been adequately shown between these differences and educational performance. For example, Labov (1969) and Stewart (1969) provide well-documented defenses of their view that the language of the black "deprived" child is linguistically and logically consistent and functional though different from the standard English dialect. In addition, they question the conclusions of earlier researchers that a nonstandard dialect is in itself an impediment to educational achievement.

Ogbu (1978) has provided a much needed cross-cultural view of the American educational system. He proposes a caste explanation for minority educational difficulties and argues that cultural deprivation and genetic inferiority explanations are inadequate. He suggests that theories which stress the social inadequacies of blacks, as well as those that stress the inadequacies of schools, ignore the system of racial castes under which blacks are forced to live and study. Comparisons are made of the educational performance of castelike minorities in six societies.

Most of the criticisms of deprivation theory highlight its methodological and theoretical shortcomings. My thesis is that the problems of the theory can be traced to social structural analysis in general. The idea that social phenomena are interrelated has prompted sociologists to generalize about problems beyond those on which they in fact have data. In Williams' words (1970: 3) they "extend by analogy."

Williams proposes that the studies of the poor usually begin with statistics on economic difficulties. In considering explanations for those difficulties the researchers turn to cultural factors. These researchers conclude that cultural disadvantage must be present if in fact there is economic impoverishment. To use Williams' terms, for researchers economic disadvantage is "extended by analogy to create a concept of cultural disadvantage."

Rather commonly, slavery is identified as the phenomenon which generated black deficits. The residues of slavery, ranging from white racist practices to self-hatred among blacks, are seen as the causes of black deficits. Hence, a review of the research on slavery should make clearer the ways in which structural approaches undergird some of the problems surrounding deprivation theory.

On the Slavery Deficit Model

Myrdal (1944), Frazier (1932, 1949, 1968) and Kardiner and Ovesey (1951) made substantial contributions to the literature on black social life. While many of their ideas have been challenged, the studies have had a great impact on all areas of race relations research, including cultural deprivation research. It is my contention that certain identifiable social structural assumptions guided these researchers and their development of models for the analysis of black America. Therefore, in seeking to outline the approaches taken, I note the guiding principles cited by the authors themselves.

The Myrdal analysis is one of the best-documented studies of American blacks. However, many aspects of his discussion reveal some social structural ideas. For example, he proposes the concept of "vicious cycle" to explain black inequality. In this regard he writes: "White prejudice and discrimination keep the Negro low in standards of living, health, education, manners and morals. This in turn, gives support to white prejudice. White prejudice and Negro standards thus mutually 'cause' each other" (1944: 74).

In refuting the idea of the primacy of the economic factors, he says: "There still exists, however, another theoretical idea which is similar to the idea of panacea: the idea that there is *one* predominant factor. Usually the so-called 'economic' factor is assumed to be the basic factor. . . . As we look upon the problem of dynamic social causation, this approach is unrealistic and narrow. We do not, deny the conditions under which Negroes are allowed to earn a living are tremendously important for their welfare. *But these conditions are closely interrelated to all other conditions of Negro* life" (1944: 77–78, emphasis added).

Frazier, too, wrestled with the question: How central are economic forces in black life? One finds in his writings the argument that "sociological analysis must include economic and political factors relevant to the analysis of a particular system of social relations which is being studied" (Frazier, 1968:5). Frazier sets forth a "logical" rather than a "chronological" scheme for the study of racial problems. Through the use of such a model for the study of the black family, he argues that few African mating and sexual patterns had a bearing on New World black family patterns, and that the Negro family under slavery acquired the "character of a natural organization in that it was based primarily upon human impulses and individual wishes rather than upon law and mores (1944: 193).

For Frazier, economic and political factors set into motion during slavery have influenced black social institutions. In a study of The Negro Family in Chicago (1932) and in later studies, Frazier applies his model of social structure and race relations to the study of black family patterns. In general, it can be said that he attributed twentieth-century black family disorganization to the institution of slavery and to the disruptive influences of urbanization. He uses various historical studies of slavery to support his view of its destructive, deculturating effects.

Kardiner and Ovesey, psychiatrists, conducted one of the earliest and most systematic studies of the personality of the black American (The Mark of Oppression, 1951). They argue that there has been a fragmentation of the social life of man by the social sciences and propose a more holistic approach. Then, accepting a view of slavery which holds that little of African culture survived in the New World (reliance upon work of E. Franklin Frazier), they propose the following as psychological effects of slave status (1951:47):

(1) Degradation of self-esteem.
(2) Destruction of cultural forms and forced adoption of foreign cultural traits.
(3) Destruction of the family unit with particular disparagement of the male.
(4) Relative enhancement of the female status, thus making her the central figure in the culture, by virtue of her value to the white male for sexual ends and as a mammy to the white children.
(5) The destruction of social cohesion among Negroes by the inability to have their own culture.

(6) The idealization of the white master; but with this ideal was incorporated an object which was at once revered and hated. These became incompatible constitutents of the Negro personality.

Further, the authors see self-hatred and low self-esteem as being constantly reinforced by racism and oppression. The economic conditions under which blacks live are cited as a continuing source of self-hatred.

Interwoven into the prologue of the analysis are assumptions about the extent to which slavery destroyed black cultural values and on the connection between family life and personality difficulties. The idea that the parts of the black psyche are incompatible is the main theme of the study. Finally, in concluding their study the authors state ''that the Negro lacks the capacity for social cohesion has been noted by many observers.'' (1951: 359).

These sources suggest two conclusions relevant here: (1) slavery has led to pathology, low standards and deficits among blacks; and (2) deficits in one area of black life inevitably affect other areas and cause them similarly to be deficient.

With reference to the first, the view is that slavery, with its processes of ''destructuration'' of African social-cultural institutions was and continues to be a major barrier to the ''restructuration'' of contemporary black American society. According to this position, slavery has put an almost indelible mark on all black social institution and on the black jpsyche. Thus, slavery provides a ''logical'' and satisfying historical-structural explanation for the present deficits of blacks.

Challenges to the Slavery Deficit Model

The conclusions can be criticized on both empirical and theoretical grounds. Among historians and others who have studied American slavery there is considerable debate over the exact nature of slavery as an institution and its impact on black life and culture. Herskovits (1941) in a pioneering critical study challenged the idea of the complete deculturation of New World blacks. He showed that many Africanisms persisted despite slavery. Recent works by Fogel and Engerman (1974), Genovese (1974), David et al. (1976), and Lane (1971) continue the debate. These studies question the proposition that slavery altered black familial and sexual patterns, dehumanized slaves, and contributed to the economy of the American South. As in the case of black family studies, much of the debate now centers on the availability and adequacy of quantitative data for re-evaluating various theories.

Other examples can be drawn from almost every area of race relations theory and research. Grier and Cobbs (1968) offer a view on the effects of slavery that differs from the position taken by Kardiner and Ovesey. Moreover, the latter study has been attacked on methodological grounds, the attack sometimes stressing the fact that the results were based on a limited sample.

Even if slavery had important economic consequences for blacks, one cannot conclude that all other aspects of life likewise were impaired. There is reason to question these three arguments which crop up in the literature: (1) that slavery destroyed black social life; (2) that the structural patterns engendered by slavery have persisted; and (3) that the effects of these structural patterns have affected negatively black educational performance.

Having concluded from historical studies of slavery and contemporary analyses that blacks have experienced and still experience varying degrees of economic and political inequality, social scientists exploring other areas of life appear to have concluded a priori that similar deficiencies must exist in other areas of social life. As a result, deficit models have been applied to the study of black kinship structure, value systems, language, the psyche and additional social and psychological properties. It is a conceptual leap, not empirically grounded theory which accounts for the transfer of the deprivation theme from one part of the "social structure" to another.

CONCLUSIONS

Critics of deficit theory have made two important observations: (1) the debate on deprivation centers more on models and concepts than on empirical evidence; and (2) much of the support for the theory is ideological and political. However, little attention has been paid to the metatheoretical basis of deficit models, the concern of this paper. Even less attention has been paid to the process by which ideological and value orientations are converted into theoretical propositions. Consequently, many critics have oversimplified the process for abandoning deficit theory. Often an *ad hominem* approach is taken in which the problem is depicted as the pre-eminence of biased researchers.

Deficit theorizing is not merely the result of the ethnocentric perceptions of an individual researcher or of his political ideas. It is also the result of certain assumptions made by structural analysts. My purpose has not been to explore in detail the empirical inadequacies of deprivation theory; nor would I call for the abandonment of the concept of social struc ture. Indeed, almost no serious social scientists would argue that there is *no* relationship among the various parts of society. It is clear, however, that only carefully designed empirical studies aimed at exploring and measuring possible interrelations will help answer some of the questions structural approaches pose. In the absence of such systematic analyses, many of the conclusions in the literature are unwarranted.

The existence of a logically consistent model is merely the beginning of scientific research. The assessment of the nature and extent of the interrelationships among the parts of the social structure cannot merely be assumed at the level of metatheory or at the level of substantive theory. They must be demonstrated emprically. This does not mean that one must abandon conceptualizing, theorizing and pre-investigatory model building for a crass empiricism. Such would only add to the already extreme emphasis on "nontheoretical" quantitative analysis which characterizes so much of contemporary social science. Instead, efforts must be made to examine and make more explicit the conceptual model, or theory, one uses in research and to examine more closely the fit between model and data.

Empirical analyses need not be limited to the accumulation of quantitative data alone. Many valid qualitative approaches may be taken. In the area of cultural deprivation theorizing such data would be useful to test propositions that deficits in one social structural part lead to deficits in other parts. For example, one must seek to ascertain whether particular patterns of economic deficit are highly correlated with patterns of family structure and whether this family structure is linked to poor educational performance. Since correlations alone, especially those between very delimited indices, are not evidence of causation, more broadly based analyses than those frequently used must be attempted.

As this analysis of the basis of cultural deprivation theory also suggests, it may be necessary to move beyond a critique of substantive theory and methods alone. It may be necessary to re-examine at the level of metatheory many of the premises and assumptions which underlie all of social science research, including the concept of "social structure" itself, as Boudon (1968) and Homans (1975) have proposed. Such a re-examination must proceed at both the conceptual and empirical levels of analysis. That is, one must critique both the logical consistency and the empirical grounding of the social structural assumption of deprivation theory.

I tend to share the opinion of Homans (1975:55) that it may not be accurate to conclude, as many advocates of the social structural view have tended to do, that the interrelations of the various parts of the social structure with one another "dampen the variation that is possible in any one of them." Much more variation may be possible within social structural boundaries than sometimes is assumed by social researchers.

For example, just as it has been suggested that modernization need not always affect all societies in the same way, parts of a given society may be differentially affected by modernization trends. In a similar vein, many anthropologists have long ago noted that "sophisticated" development in the technological and economic arenas of a soceity may not always be accompanied by similar levels of development in other parts of the society, and vice versa. Indeed, Maruyama (1968) proposes a more elaborate, cybernetic conceptual model of the evolutionary development of societies to replace the older, systems model which underlies social structural conceptions. He suggests that such a model may better account for societal variations.

Thus, it may well be that black Americans and others labeled "deprived," though having experienced and continuing to experience economic and political deficits, may have maintained much variation in other areas of social life. This variation may include aspects of what have been labeled "deficits" as well as aspects of "nondeficits." It may also be argued that the "deficit" label may be inappropriately applied to noneconomic arenas where group differences are not as easily quantifiable. Few analysts would apply such a label to cultural and societal differences in artistic expression, religion, philosophy, etc. By what standards, for example, would one determine the deficiency of African musical expression in comparison to European expression? Can one argue convincingly on a scientific basis that non-Christian religions are more deficient than Christianity? Similarly, many researchers have also questioned the extent to which differing family patterns, personality traits, dialects, etc., may be given "deficit" and "nondeficit" labels (i.e., on the basis of any standards other than that of the power of the labeler).

This is not to argue for a beneficent view of racial oppression and economic exploitation in the United States, historically or presently. For example, this charge has been made against Fogel and Engerman (1974) and Gutman (1976). Critics have suggested that the authors have offered another form of apology for slavery and the oppression of blacks by overstressing the beneficent aspects of slavery. It is absurd to think that the persisting economic and political oppression and the concomitant powerlessness of blacks and the poor have not had some impact on various aspects of social life. Rather, I am suggesting that an alternative, more skeptical model which does not automatically assume deficits to exist in all parts of the society of those labeled deprived may provide a more scientific tool for research. Such a skeptical model better fits the present level of empirical grounding in this area of research. Such a revised model for the study of blacks and the poor in American society may also be a more useful model for directing sound social change efforts, an approach advocated by Coleman (1971). Attempts at change would be directed at "real" areas of deficit rather than being dispersed and consequently ineffective.

Finally, the focus in this paper on scientific methodological concerns related to cultural deprivation theorizing must not obscure the role of ideology on social scientific research. That is, we must not neglect analysis of the larger societal determinants of much of deprivation theory outlined earlier in this analysis. The use of the terms "deficit" and "deprivation" represents a political-ideological stance and emanates from certain political realities of American and modern capitalist society as many critics have noted. In many respects labels of deficiency are often used by the powerful to describe and "explain" the status of the powerless (on this point see Blauner, 1972).

Much of the affinity for cultural deprivation theory and the leap that is taken may reside in functionalist analysis. Gouldner (1970), among others, has noted the tendency for American social science to center around conservative, functionalist explanations for social reality. In other words, the dominance of functionalist theory might have contributed to the formulation of deprivation theory. This might have occurred because of the following. First, a systems approach and an emphasis on interdependency are integral to functionalist theory. Second, deprivation may parallel dysfunction, a central notion in functionalist theory.

In discussing the role of extrasocial science influences on social research, Taylor et al. (1974: 31) say:

> We wish to remove ourselves from that comfortable school of thought which believes that theories compete with each other in some scholarly limbo, heuristic facility being the only test of survival. We need to explain why certain theories, despite their manifest inability to come to terms with their subject matter, survive and indeed . . . flourish.

Theory building and testing, and social science research in general, is a scholarly and scientific venture. It is also shaped and channeled by the many economic, political, social and other forces within American society. Although in many instances we need to look at those forces to understand the attractiveness of given theories, some models, including the deficit model, would appear to be the product of ideas internal—and indeed basic—to the social sciences.

REFERENCES

Allen, Walter
  1978   "The search for applicable theories of Black family life." Journal of Marriage and the Family 40: 117–129.
Baratz, Joan C.
  1969   "Teaching reading in an urban Negro school system." In Joan C. Baratz and Robert Shuy (eds.), Teaching Black Children to Read. Wash. D.C.: Center for Applied Statistics.
Baratz, Stephen and Baratz, Joan
  1970   "Early childhood intervention: the science basis of institutional racism." In Cashdan et al. (eds.) Language and Education. London: Routledge and Kegan Paul.
Billingsley, Andrew
  1968   Black Families in White America. Englewood Cliffs, N.J.: Prentice-Hall.
Blauner, Robert
  1972   Racial Oppression in America. New York: Harper and Row.
Boudon, Raymond
  1968   "A quoi sert la notion de structure?" Paris: Gallimard.
Coleman, James S.
  1971   Resources for Social Change: Race in the United States. New York: John Wiley and Sons.
Coser, Lewis A.
  1975   "Structure and conflict." Pp. 210–219 in Peter M. Blau (ed.), Approaches to the Study of Social Structure.
Dave, Ravindrakumar H.
  1963   The Identification and Measurement of Environmental Process Variables that are Related to Educational Achievement. Doctor's Thesis, Chicago: University of Chicago.
David, Paul A. et al.
  1976   Reckoning with Slavery. New York: Oxford University Press.
Fogel, Robert W. and Engerman, Stanley L.
  1974   Time on the Cross: The Economics of American Negro Slavery. Boston: Little Brown and Company.
Frazier, E. Franklin
  1932   The Negro Family in Chicago. Chicago: University of Chicago Press.
Frazier, E. Franklin
  1949   "Race contacts and the social structures." American Sociological Review 14: 1–11.
Frazier, E. Franklin
  1968   E. Franklin Frazier on Race Relations, edited by G. Franklin Edwards. Chicago: University of Chicago Press.

Genovese, Eugene D.
  1974   Roll, Jordan Roll: The World the Slaves Made. New York: Pantheon Books.
Ginsburg, Herbert
  1972   The Myth of the Deprived Child: Poor Children and Education. Englewood
         Cliffs, N.J.: Prentice-Hall.
Goode, William J.
  1975   ''Homans' and Mertons' structural approach.'' in Peter M. Blau (ed.), Ap-
         proaches to the Study of Social Structure. New York: The Free Press.
Gordon, Edmund
  1965   ''Characteristics of socially disadvantaged children.'' The Review of Educa-
         tional Research 35: 377–388.
Gouldner, Alvin
  1970   The Coming Crisis of Western Sociology. New York: Basic Books.
Grier, William H. and Cobbs, Price M.
  1968   Black Rage. New York: Basic Books.
Gutman, Herbert G.
  1976   The Black Family in Slavery and Freedom: 1750–1925. New York: Pantheon.
Herskovits, Melville J.
  [1941] The Myth of the Negro Past. Boston: Beacon Press.
  1958
Hill, Robert
  1971   The Strengths of Black Families. New York: Emerson Hall.
Hofstadter, Richard
  1944   Social Darwinism in American Thought. Boston: Beacon Press.
Homans, George C.
  1975   ''What do we mean by social 'structure'?'' Pp. 53–65 in Peter M. Blau (ed.),
         Approaches to the Study of Social Structure. New York: Free Press.
Kardiner, Abram and Ovesey, Lionel
  1951   The Mark of Oppression. Cleveland: World Publishing Co.
Keddie, Nell
  1973   The Myth of Cultural Deprivation. Harmondsworth, Middlesex, England: Pen-
         guin Books.
Kuhn, Thomas S.
  1970   The Structure of Scientific Revolution. 2nd edition, Chicago: University of
         Chicago Press.
Labov, William
  1969   The Logic of Nonstandard English. Washington, D.C.: Georgetown Mono-
         graphs on Language and Linguistics 22: 1–31; also in Keddie (1973).
Lane, Ann J.
  1971   The Debate over Slavery: Stanley Elkins and His Critics. Urbana: University of
         Illinois Press.
Lewis, Oscar
  1959   Five Families: Mexican Case Studies in the Culture of Poverty. New York:
         Basic Books.
Maruyama, Magoraoh
  1968   ''The second cybernetics: deviation-amplifing mutual causal processes.'' Pp.
         304–313 in Walter Buckley (ed.), Modern System Research for the Behavioral
         Scientist. Chicago: Aldine Publishing Co.

Miller, S. M.
1964 "The American lower class: a typological approach." Social Research 1: 1–22.
Myrdal, Gunnar
1944 An American Dilemma: The Negro Problem and Modern Democracy. Vols. I
      and II. New York: Harper and Row.
Ogbu, John U.
1978 Minority Education and Caste: The American System in Cross Cultural Perspec-
      tive. New York: Academic Press.
Riessman, Frank
1962 The Culturally Deprived Child. New York: Harper and Row.
Ryan, William
1971 Blaming the Victim. New York: Pantheon.
Scanzoni, John.
1971 The Black Family in Modern Society. Boston: Allyn and Bacon.
Stewart, William A.
1969 "Sociopolitical issues in the treatment of Negro dialect" and "Historical and
      structural bases for the recognition of Negro dialect." In James E. Alatis (ed.),
      Monograph Series on Languages and Linguistics 22. Washington, D.C.:
      Georgetown University.
Taylor, Ian, Walton, Paul and Young, Jack
1974 The New Criminology, 2nd edition. New York: Harper and Row.
————.
1975 Critical Criminology. London: Routledge and Kegan Paul.
Valentine, Charles A.
1968 Culture and Poverty: Critique and Counter Proposals. Chicago: University Press
      of Chicago.
Valentine, Charles and Valentine, Bettylou
1975 "Brain damage and the intellectual defense of inequality." Current Anthropol-
      ogy 16: 117–150.
Williams, Frederick
1970 Language and Poverty: Perspectives on a Theme. Chicago: Markham.

AUTHOR INDEX

SUBJECT INDEX

Africans
  as racial group, 23, 30
  suicide among, 57
affirmative action, 108, 111, 112
anomie
  and suicide, 57
  in Switzerland, 81, 84
ascription, 81, 97–98, 112
assimilation, ix, 10, 82, 84
  of French immigrants, 120, 121

Black Americans, 31, 118, 129, 134, 146
  and discrimination, 101, 108
  and education, 6, 62, 65, 110, 140
  and employment, 108, 109, 110
  attitudes toward, 109
  compared with French Canadians, 118–120,
    128–129

bourgeoisie in Canada, 121, 124, 125
British Canadians, *see* English Canadians
British North American Act, 121
British Race Relations Act (1976), 36, 37

caste, 99–100
  in India, (*see also* India) 98, 100–101, 103,
    112
  in the United States, 101, 109, 140
Catholic
  Church in Canadian society, 117, 118, 126
  workers and immigration to Switzerland, 92
class, *see* social class
culture
  and deprivation, 133–134, 136–141, 145, 147
  of poverty, 136

dependent societies, 116–117, 124, 129, 130

155

Research in Race and Ethnic Relations

A Research Annual

Series Editors: **Cora Bagley Marrett**
University of Wisconsin — Madison
Cheryl B. Leggon
*University of Illinois
— Chicago Circle.*

The contributions to this series consist of original research papers from an international community of specialists on race and ethnic relations. The purpose of the series is to explore recent theoretical and empirical developments in the field. Each volume will be organized around a particular theme. The first volume is focused on efforts to link specific empirical questions with broader theoretical issues. Specifically, the contributors present theoretical perspectives they have found useful in their own work, discuss the state of their work using such perspectives, and outline the kinds of additional research they deem essential for building the given theories or frameworks.

Volume 1.   **Published 1979**   **Cloth**   **Institutions: $ 29.50**
ISBN 0-89232-064-8   **199 pages**   **Individuals: $ 14.75**

CONTENTS. Preface. Introduction. Theoretical Perspectives on Race and Ethnic Relations: A Socio-Historical Approach, *Cheryl B. Leggon, University of Illinois - Chicago Circle.* **The Past, Present and Future of Split Labor Market Theory,** *Edna Bonacich, University of California - Riverside.* **Race Relations from Liberal, Black and Marxist Perspectives,** *Dennis Forsythe, University of the West Indies.* **Ethnicity and Class in a Plural Society: Nigeria.** *Onigu Otite, University of Ibadan.* **Military Organization in Multi-Ethnically Segmented Societies,** *J. 'Bayo Adekson, University of Ibadan.* **Self-Esteem as a Pivotal Concept in Race and Ethnic Relations,** *Christopher Bagley, University of Surrey.* **The Social Psychology of Riot Participation,** *Marguerite Bryan, Xavier University of New Orleans.* **Author/Subject Index.**

JAI PRESS INC., P.O. Box 1678, 165 West Putnam Avenue,
Greenwich, Connecticut 06830.

Telephone: 203-661-7602   Cable Address: JAIPUBL

Research in Economic Anthropology

A Research Annual

Series Editor: **George Dalton**
Departments of Economics and Anthropology
Northwestern University.

REVIEWS: "...responding to converging interests in several disciplines in the economic operation and development of preindustrial societies, both before and after Western expansion. The contributions...by eminent anthropologists, economists, and historians are of uniformly high quality and, whether empirical essays or not, have significant theoretical implications...Recommended to academic libraries in colleges and universities where there are anthropologists and other social scientists interested in comparative and developmental economic." — *Choice*

"...recommended to all sociologists working in the field of rural development." — *Sociologia Ruralis*

Volume 1.	**Published 1978**	**Cloth**	**Institutions:**	**$ 32.00**
ISBN 0-89232-040-9		**338 pages**	**Individuals:**	**$ 16.00**

CONTENTS: Introduction, *George Dalton.* **The Origins of Money,** *Philip Grierson, Cambridge University.* **Slaves, Trade and Taxes: The Material Basis of Political Power in Pre-Colonial West Africa,** *Robin Law, University of Stirling, Scotland,* **Factors of Production, Economic Circulation and Inequality in Inner Arabia,** *Fredrik Barth, University of Oslo.* **"Finance and Production" Revisited: In Pursuit of a Comparison,** *Andrew Strathern, University College-London.* **Exchange as Structure, Or Why Doesn't Everybody Eat His Own Pigs,** *Abraham Rosman and Paula G. Rubel, Barnard College of Columbia University.* **The Impact of Colonization on Aboriginal Economies in Stateless Societies,** *George Dalton, Northwestern University.* **The Economic Basis of Tallensi Social History in the Early Twentieth Century,** *Keith Hart, Yale University.* **The Destructive Consequences of Peasant Culture in Modern Italy,** *Carlo Tullio-Altan, University of Florence.* **Patterns of Market Expansion in the Nineteenth Century: A Quantitative Study,** *Irma Adelman, University of Maryland, and Cynthia Taft Morris, American University.* **Socialism and Economic Growth,** *W. Arthur Lewis, Princeton University.*

Volume 2.	**Published 1979**	**Cioth**	**Institutions:**	**$ 32.00**
ISBN 0-89232-085-0		**390 pages**	**Individuals:**	**$ 16.00**

CONTENTS: Introduction, *George Dalton.* **The Golden Stool and the Elephant Tail: An Essay on Wealth in Asante,** *Ivor Wilks, Northwestern University.* **Pre-Colonial Gold Mining and the State in the Akan Region, With a Critique of the Terray Hypothesis,** *Raymond E. Dumett, Purdue University.* **The Political Economy of Dahomey,** *K.P. Moseley, Brooklyn College.* **Rural Periodic Markets in Roman North Africa as Mechanisms of Social Integration and Control,** *Brent D. Shaw, University of Lethbridge.* **Some Early German Contributions to Economic Anthropology,** *Jasper Koecke, Northwestern University.* **The Impact of Christianity on a Melanesian Economy,** *Stuart Berde, University of Massachusetts-Boston.* **Enlargement of the Exchange Economy in Tropical Africa,** *United Nations (1954).* **A Theory of Development Strategy for Equitable Growth in Developing Countries,** *Irma Adelman, University of California-Berkeley.* **On Land Disputes in Eastern Turkey,** *Nur Yalman, Harvard University.* **The Effects of Reservation Bordertowns and Energy Exploitation on American Indian Economic Development,** *Nancy J. Owens, Northern Cheyenne Research Project.* **Criteria for Choosing Successful Homesteaders in Brazil,** *Emelio F. Moran, Indiana University.* **The Socio-Economics of Ranching in Kenya,** *Ian Livingston, University of East Anglia.*

Volume 3.   Published 1980   Cloth   Institutions: $ 35.00
ISBN 0-89232-114-8   400 pages   Individuals: $ 17.50

CONTENTS: **Introduction,** George Dalton, Northwestern University. **The Silent Trade,** P.J. Hamilton Grierson. **On Silent Trade,** John A. Price, York University, Toronto. **Silent Trade in Japan,** Shinichiro Kurimoto, Nara Prefectural College. **Ports of Trade in Nineteenth Century Bali,** Clifford Geertz, Institute for Advanced Study at Princeton. **Applied Anthropology (1930).** A.R. Radcliffe-Brown. **The Encomienda and the Gensis of a Colonial Economy in Spanish America,** Robert G. Keith, Harvard University. **Growth and Improverishment in the Middle of the Nineteenth Century,** Irma Adelman, University of California, Berkeley, and Cynthia Taft Morris, The American University. **Sharecropping in Kelantan, Malaysia,** F.A. Bray and A.F. Robertson, University of Cambridge. **Development Planning in Niger: Techniques of Regional Analysis,** Arjaan Everts, Advisor in Regional Planning, Republic of Niger. **The Gezira Development Project in Sudan,** Sarah P. Voll, Consultant, Cairo. **Employment Opportunity and Migration among the Mossi of Upper Volta,** Gregory A. Finnegan, Lake Forest College, Illinois. **Political Ecology of Fishing in Japan,** Harumi Befu, Stanford University. **A Community Approach to Aggregate Demographic Patterns in Rural Turkey,** Samuel S. Lieberman, The Population Council, New York.

Volume 4.   Spring 1981   Cloth   Institutions' $ 32.00
ISBN 0-89232-189-X   Ca. 325 pages   Individuals: $ 16.00

CONTENTS: **Introduction,** George Dalton. **Economic Anthropology and History: The Work of Karl Polanyi,** L. Valensi, W.G. L. Randles, J.P. Chretien, A. Margarido and N. Wachtel. **Life Paradigms: Makassae (East Timor) Views of Production, Reproduction and Exchange,** Shepard Forman, The Ford Foundation. **Integrated Community Development: Vicos in Peru,** Ulrich Koehler, Universitaet Muenster. **The Impact in Peru of the Vicos Project,** James R. Himes, The Ford Foundation. **Land Tenure in a Brazilian Community: Life Cycle Patterns and Intergenerational Comparisons,** John Steele, U.S. Department of Agriculture and Don Kanel, University of Wisconsin-Madison. **Agriculture and Community in Maharashtra, India,** Lee Schlesinger, University of North Carolina-Chapel Hill. **Farm Management as Cultural Style: Studies in Adaptive Process in the North American Agrifamily,** John W. Bennett, Washington University.

The Economic Organization of the Inka State

John V. Murra
Cornell University and
Institute of Andean Research.

Supplement 1 to Research in Economic Anthropology

Published 1980   Cloth   Institutions: $ 32.00
ISBN 0-89232-118-0   214 pages   Individuals: $ 16.00

CONTENTS: **Foreword,** George Dalton. **Introduction,** John V. Murra. **Part One: Agriculture. Land Tenures. Herds and Herders. Cloth. Preliminary Summary. Part Two: Peasant Corvee and the Revenues of the State. The Disposal of Surplus or the Redistributive State. Barter and Trade. From Corvee to Retainership. Finale. Glossary. Bibliography. Index.**

JAI PRESS INC., P.O. Box 1678, 165 West Putnam Avenue, Greenwich, Connecticut 06830.

Telephone: 203-661-7602   Cable Address: JAIPUBL

Political Power and Social Theory

A Research Annual

Series Editor: **Maurice Zeitlin**
Department of Sociology
University of California
— Los Angeles.

Guest Editors: **Gosta Esping-Andersen**
Department of Sociology
Harvard University

Roger Friedland
Department of Sociology
University of California —
Santa Barbara.

| Volume 3. | Fall 1981 | Cloth | Institutions: $ 31.00 |
| ISBN 0-89232-204-7 | | Ca. 375 pages | Individuals: $ 15.50 |

CONTENTS: Class Coalitions in the Making of West European Economics, *Gosta Esping-Andersen, Harvard University and Roger Friedland, University of California-Santa Barbara.* **French Unions Face the 1980's: The CGT and the CFDT in the Strategic Conflicts and Economic Crisis in Contemporary France,** *George Ross, Carleton University.* **The Italian Communist Party and the Social Movements, 1968-1975,** *Marzio Barbagli and Piergiorgio Corbetta, Universita Degli Studi di Bologna.* **Local Government Control and the Political Strategy of the European Communist Parties,** *Paoli Ceccarelli, University of Venice.* **When is the Time Ripe? A Question to the Commission on the 1975 Social Democratic Party Program,** *Sten Johansson, Swedish Institute for Social Research.* **Class Conflict and the Socialdemocratic Reform Cycle in Germany,** *Mary Nolan, Harvard University and Charles Sabel, Massachusetts Institute of Technology.* **Class Compromises in Advanced Capitalism: Social Democracy vs Econocommunism,** *Mark Kesselman, Columbia University.* **The Labor Movement, Political Power and Workers Participation in Western Europe,** *Evelyne Huber Stephens, College of the Holy Cross and John Stephens, Brown University.* **The Servicing Work of Women and the Capitalist State,** *Laura Balbo, Center for European Studies, Cambridge, Mass.* **Structure and Sequences of Nuclear Energy Politics,** *Herbert Kischelt, University of Bielefeld.* **The Politics of Growth and Recession in Western Europe,** *Iannos Papantoniu, OECD, Paris.* **Author/Subject Index.**

INSTITUTIONAL STANDING ORDERS will be granted a 10% discount and be filled automatically upon publication. Please indicate initial volume of standing order
INDIVIDUAL ORDERS must be prepaid by personal check or credit card. Please include $1.50 per volume for postage and handling.
Please encourage your library to subscribe to this series.

JAI PRESS INC., P.O. Box 1678, 165 West Putnam Avenue,
Greenwich, Connecticut 06830.

Telephone: 203-661-7602   Cable Address: JAIPUBL

Research in the Interweave of Social Roles: Women and Men

A Research Annual

Series Editors: **Helena Znaniecka Lopata**
Center for Comparative Study of Social Roles
Loyola University, Chicago

David R. Maines
The Program on Women,
Northwestern University.

| Volume 1. | Published 1980 | Cloth | Institutions: $ 32.00 |
| ISBN 0-89232-066-4 | 325 pages | | Individuals: $ 16.00 |

INSTITUTIONAL STANDING ORDERS *will be granted a 10% discount and be filled automatically upon publication. Please indicate initial volume of standing order*
INDIVIDUAL ORDERS *must be prepaid by personal check or credit card. Please include $1.50 per volume for postage and handling.*
Please encourage your library to subscribe to this series.

JAI PRESS INC., P.O. Box 1678, 165 West Putnam Avenue, Greenwich, Connecticut 06830.

Telephone: 203-661-7602   Cable Address: JAIPUBL